DISASTERS, FIRES, AND RESCUES 4

DANIEL S. KNOWLES

Copyright © 2019 Daniel S. Knowles

All rights reserved. No part of this publication may be reproduced, distributed, or transmitted in any form or by any means, including photocopying, recording, or other electronic or mechanical methods, without the prior written permission of the publisher, except in the case of brief quotations embodied in critical reviews and certain other noncommercial uses permitted by copyright law. For permission requests, write to the publisher, addressed "Attention: Permissions Coordinator," at the address below.

Zeta Publishing, Inc
3850 SE 58th Ave
Ocala, FL 34480
www.zetapublishing.com

Ordering Information:
Quantity sales. Special discounts are available on quantity purchases by corporations, associations, and others. For details, contact the publisher at the address above.
Orders by U.S. trade bookstores and wholesalers. Please contact Zeta Publishing: Tel: (352) 694-2553; Fax: (352) 694-1791 or visit www.zetapublishing.com

Rev. Date: March 2019

ISBN: 978-1-950340-04-0 (sc)
ISBN: 978-1950340-05-7 (e)

Library of Congress: 2019934597
Printed in the United States of America

DISASTERS, FIRES, AND RESCUES 4

THIS PET SNAKE NAMED CHARLES RIDES THE FIRE ENGINE AND MOST OF THE TIME ON THE FRONT BUMPER

BY DANIEL S. KNOWLES

County police in Rockville narrowed their investigation of one of the worst fires in a decade to two juveniles this week and arrested the youths in connection with the burning of the historic Liberty Milling Co. Granary in Germantown.

The five-story granary was destroyed by the Saturday afternoon blaze that brought more than 33 fire trucks and 100 firemen from as far away as Silver Spring to save the structure. Firemen battled the blaze for hours, and contended with smoke and spark problems well into the next day in what one fire official recalled as "the only four-alarm/two-specials fire in the county in 10 years."

The granary had been a county landmark since 1918 when it was built on the site of yet another mill that was destroyed by fire in 1912. Recently it was used for sparse warehouse storage.

Three firemen suffered minor injuries in the blaze that brought 14 engine companies and four hook-and-ladder trucks responding to the alarm. Firemen had to lay water supply pipes from as far away as one mile to extinguish it.

The heat caused extreme damage to adjacent silos, causing the collapse of two of them, charred the roofs of nearby farm buildings, destroyed utility poles and wires, and blew out the glass of a bank across the road. Firemen are hesitant to estimate the blaze's monetary damage, but noted the harm to adjacent buildings and poles alone would be "in the thousands."

The fire was discovered by James Lewis of Middlebrook in the afternoon, fire reports read, after he observed smoke coming from an office in the building.

Landmark Granary Burns; Two Youths Apprehended

4
DISASTERS, FIRES, AND RESCUES

BY

DANIEL S. KNOWLES

FREIGHT TRAIN WRECK IN ROCKVILLE, MD

DISASTERS, FIRES, AND RESCUES 4

By

DANIEL S. KNOWLES

WARNING

SOME OF THE PICTURES IN THIS BOOK ARE NOT VERY NICE TO LOOK AT, SO YOU MAY NOT WANT TO VIEW THEM

MULTI-ALARM PIG FIRE IN THE CITY

WHEN I WROTE AND PUT TOGETHER THIS BOOK I HAD NO INTENTIONS OF USING PICTURES SHOWING VICTIMS BODIES CUT IN PIECES, HANGING, BURNED UP IN FIRES AND WRECKS, PLANE CRASHES, TRAIN WRECKS DROWNING'S, AND JUST ALL-MESSED UP IN GENERAL. JUST NOT NICE-LOOKING ONES

HOWEVER IF I DID THAT, I WOULD NOT BE TELLING THE WHOLE STORY OR SHOWING IT, WHAT SOME FIREFIGHTERS AND OTHER EMERGENCY PERSONAL SEE EVERY DAY, AND HAVE TO DEAL WITH, IT IS ALL PART OF THEIR JOB LIKE IT OR NOT.

SO, AFTER CHANGING MY MIND, I AM GOING TO DO IT, USE SUCH PICTURES.

AGAIN IF THE PICTURES BOTHER YOU JUST DON'T LOOK AT THEM

Plane Down on the East River in New York City, NY

PLANE CRASH

TWO PERSONS ARE BURNED TO DEATH WHEN A SMALL PLANE CRASHES ON THE SAVAGE FARM IN THE EARLY 1960s

HEMP FIRESTONE A RESCUE WORKER WITH MANY YEARS OF SAVING LIVES AND PUTTING OUT FIRES WAS ALSO AN EMT, A BLT, A CPA, A PARAMEDIC, A FIREFIGHTER AND A TRAFFIC RELOCATOR. HE WAS WELL EDUCATED AND A QUALIFIED BYCYCLE CRITIC. HE ALSO WALKED DOGS SOMETIMES.

HEMP NATURALLY CARRIED DOG BISCUITS IN HIS POCKET FOR HUNGRY ANIMALS AND YOU DID NOT HAVE TO BE A DOG TO RECEIVE ONE.

HE ALSO HELPED OLD LADIES CROSS THE STREET, IF YOU DID NOT WANT TO CROSS THE STREET YOU WERE NOT HELPED

ONE DAY THE YOUNG BUCK HEMP WAS STRUCK IN HIS HEAD BY A BOLT OF LIGHTNING WHILE STROLLING ALONG ON THE SIDEWALK. HE ROLLED INTO THE STREET WITH SMOKE AND FIRE COMING

FROM HIS EARS AND MOUTH INDICATING MASSIVE DAMAGE TO HIS BRAIN

HEMP WAS RUN OVER BY A HEAVY TRUCK WHICH WAS NOT GOOD AND LATER IT WAS DETERMINED THAT HIS BRAIN HAD REWIRED AND FOR THE REST OF HIS LIFE HE WOULD TEND TO NOTICE VARIOUS ANIMALS OF ANY SIZE AND SHAPE AND TYPES AT THE SCENE OF FIRES AND ACCIDENTS THAT HE WENT ON TO ASSIST.

ALL OTHER PERSONS INCLUDING RESCUE WORKERS DID NOT SEE THESE CREATURES.

THIS BOOK SHOWS MANY OF THE CALLS THAT HEMP WENT ON, SOME SORT OF BAD BUT NOT TOO BAD. STILL IF THERE IS ANYTHING THAT BOTHERS YOU JUST DON'T LOOK AT IT.

MULTIPLE-ALARM OIL FIRE IN NEWARK NJ THAT BURNED FOR DAYS AND KILLED AT LEAST ONE VICTIM

HEMP FIRESTONE

AS A YOUNG BUCK, HEMP FIRESTONE A FORMER OWNER OF A TIRE WAREHOUSE WOULD PUT UP METAL WHEATHER VANES CONSISTING OF VARIOUS TYPES OF ANIMALS THAT WOULD SPIN AROUND AND DRAW LIGHTNING.

HEMP PUT THE ANIMALS ON HOMEOWNERS ROOFS, DOGHOUSES, TELEPHONE POLES EVEN IN SOME CASES CARS

WARNING

WARNING

IN MY CASE AFTER ALMOST 65 YEARS IN THE FIRE SERVICE YOU CAN NOT LET THIS STUFF BOTHER YOU OR GET TO SERIOUS, OR YOU WILL NOT BE ABLE TO DO YOUR JOB IN HELPING PEOPLE AND SAVING LIVES

THIS BOOK HAS PICTURES OF ACCIDENTS, FIRES, AND DISASTERS OF ALL TYPES

IT SHOWS PICTURES OF DEAD BODIES IN VARIOUS FORMS

AND SHAPES, THAT FIRST ARRIVING FIREFIGHTERS AND FIRST RESPONDERS WILL SEE

ONLY TWO OTHER DUDES KNEW ABOUT THE HEMP AND THE ANIMAL SITUATION, BURNING TREE RABBIT WHO SAW THE WHEELS OF THE PASSING TRACTOR TRAILER RUN OVER HEMPS HEAD AND RUSHED IN TO LEND A PAW AND ADMINSTER THE REQUIRED FIRST-AID AND LASTLY BUT NOT LEAST, RUNNY GOOSEFINDER, WHO WAS ALSO AT THE SCENE AND HE HAD TO RESPOND QUICKLY AND IN AN HIGHLY EFFICENT MANOR HE TOOK A BLOOD PRESSURE READING USING AN OLD BYCYCLE PUMP WHICH WAS ALL HE HAD, HAD IT NOT BEEN FOR THESE BLESSED AND DEEPLY RELIGIOUS SOULS HEMP WOULD SURELY NOT HAVE MADE IT

FATAL WRECK IN WHEATON, MD

MOTORCYCLE UNDER A BUS IN ROCKVILLE, MD 1 PERSON KILLED

AIRPLANE CRASH AT THE AIRPARK IN GAITHERSBURG

LARGE OIL FIRE IN THE BRONX IN THE 1980s

KOMODO DRAGON

RECOVERING A BODY AT GREAT FALLS, MD

WORLD'S LARGEST SIX PACK, LACROSSE, WI

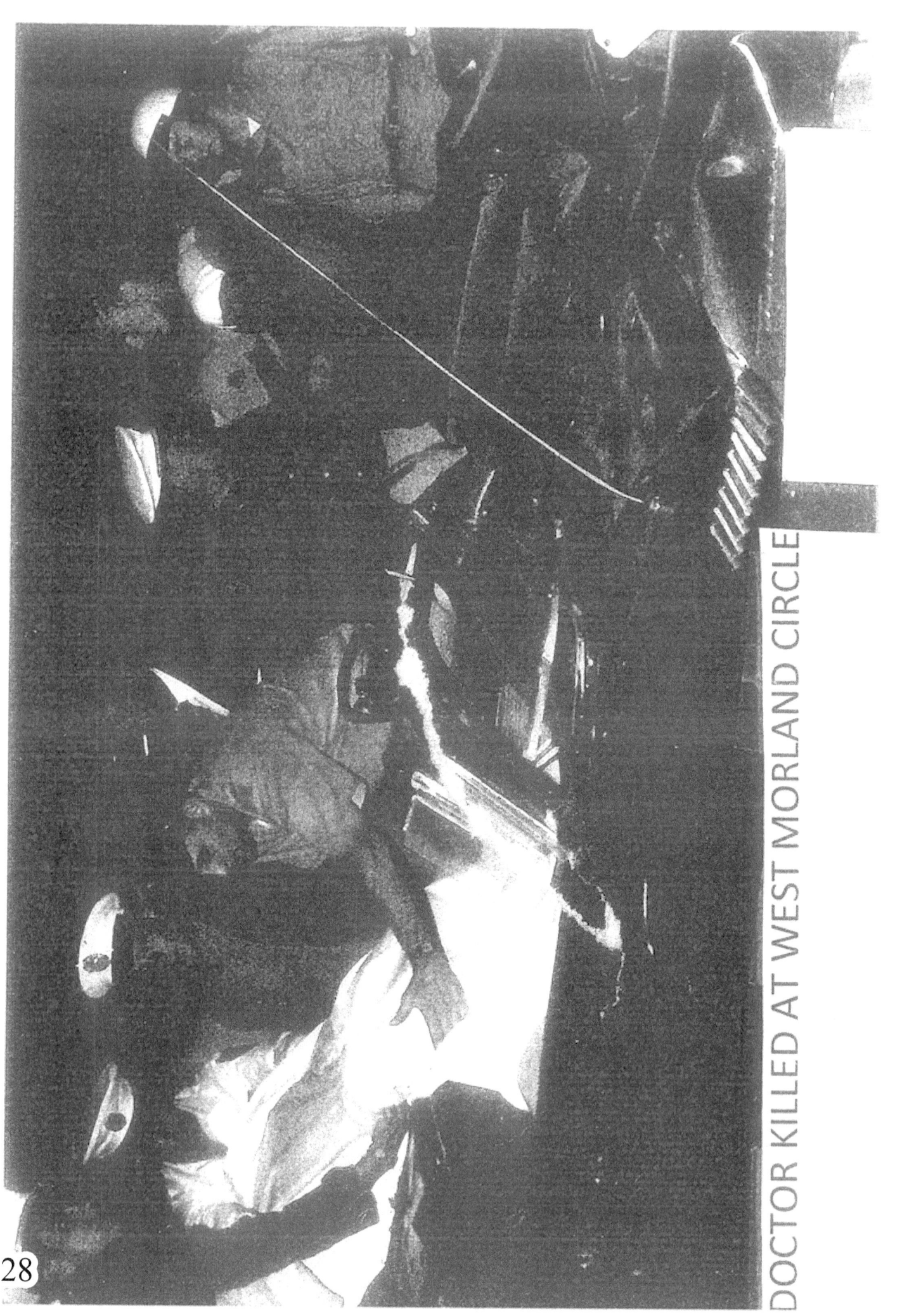

DOCTOR KILLED AT WEST MORLAND CIRCLE

CABIN JOHN FIRE CHIEF BO MONEY WATCHES AS FIREFIGHTER DANNY KNOWLES FALLS INTO THE RIVER ON TOP OF SEVERAL BODIES THAT DROWNED A WEEK EARLIER BECAUSE THEY DID NOT KNOW HOW TO SWIM

Truck ended up on top of a building

NAME THE 4 DESERTS IN THE US

(THE MOJAVE-THE SONORAN-THE GREAT BASIN-AND THE CHIHUAHUAN DESERTS

FIREFIGHTERS IN THE BRONX USING TOWER LADDERS TO RESCUE NUMEROUS PERSONS

DANNY AND CHIPPY AT THE GENERAL-ALARM OIL FIRE IN 1958 PUTTING AN ASBESTOS SUITE ON PAUL MOLE NOVEMBER 1958

THIS GUY WANTED TO KILL HIMSELF SO HE DROVE HIS CAR THROUGH THE WALL OF A NEARBY LOCAL DEPARTMENT STORE

RIP MELTON CHIEF OF THE BRANCHVILLE FD AT THE FATAL LAUREL RACETRACK FIRE THAT KILLED 3 DOZEN HORSES IN 1964

FATAL MOTORCYCLE WRECK IN GAITHERSBURG

MULTIPLE BURNED VICTIMS IN HORRIBLE WRECK ON 1-95

3 TEENS KILLED ON THE BELTWAY

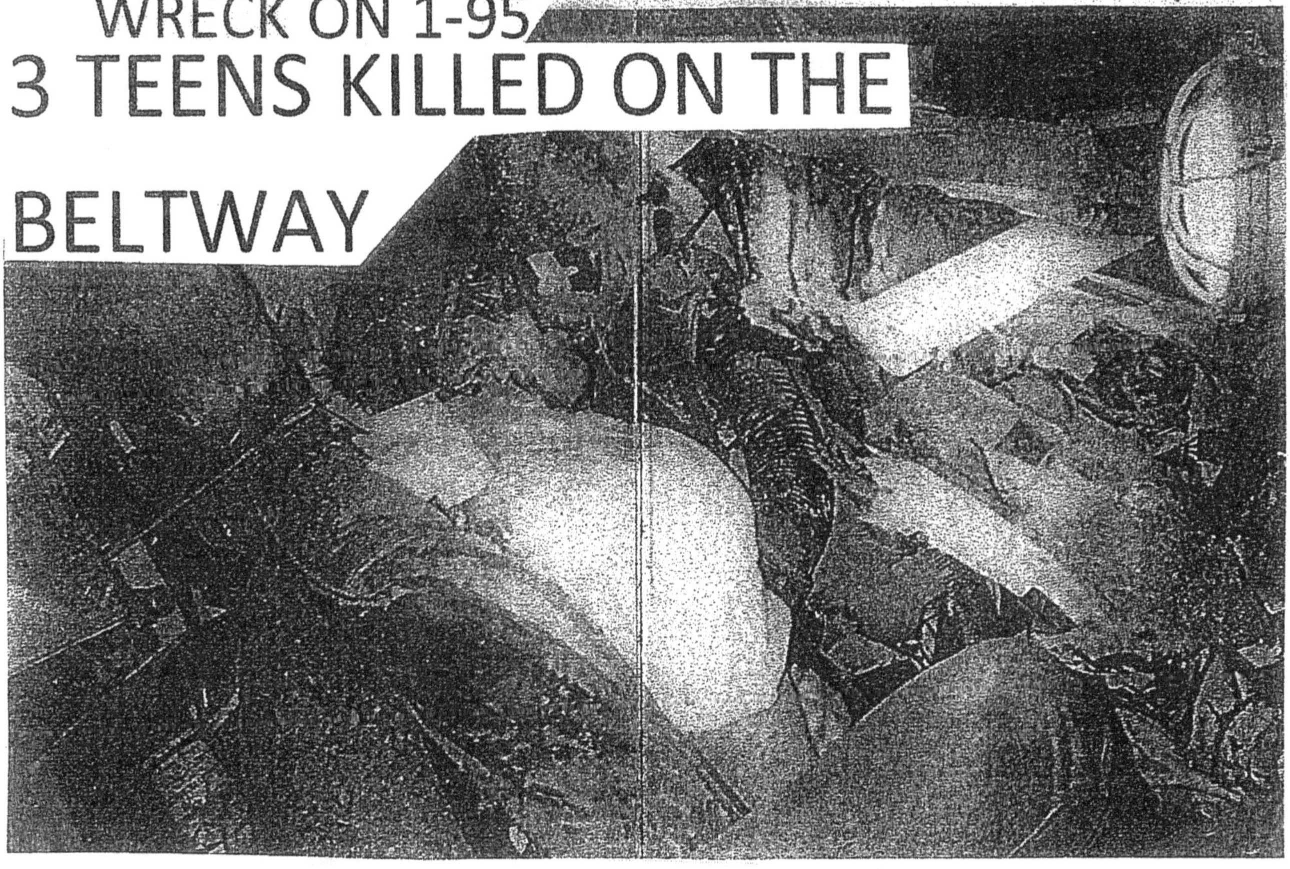

3 BURNED VICTIMS IN CAR STRUCK BY BUS

7 KILLED IN FREDRICK BUS WRECK

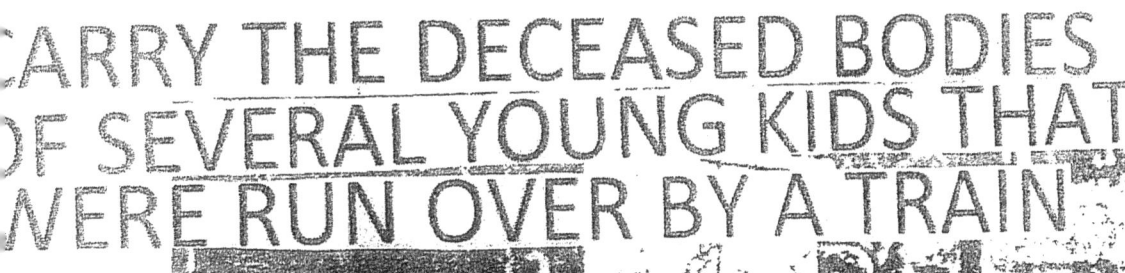

PEE WEE, AND MYSELF HELPED CARRY THE DECEASED BODIES OF SEVERAL YOUNG KIDS THAT WERE RUN OVER BY A TRAIN

FATAL APARTMENT FIRE IN THE BRONX, ONE DOG FOUND ALIVE

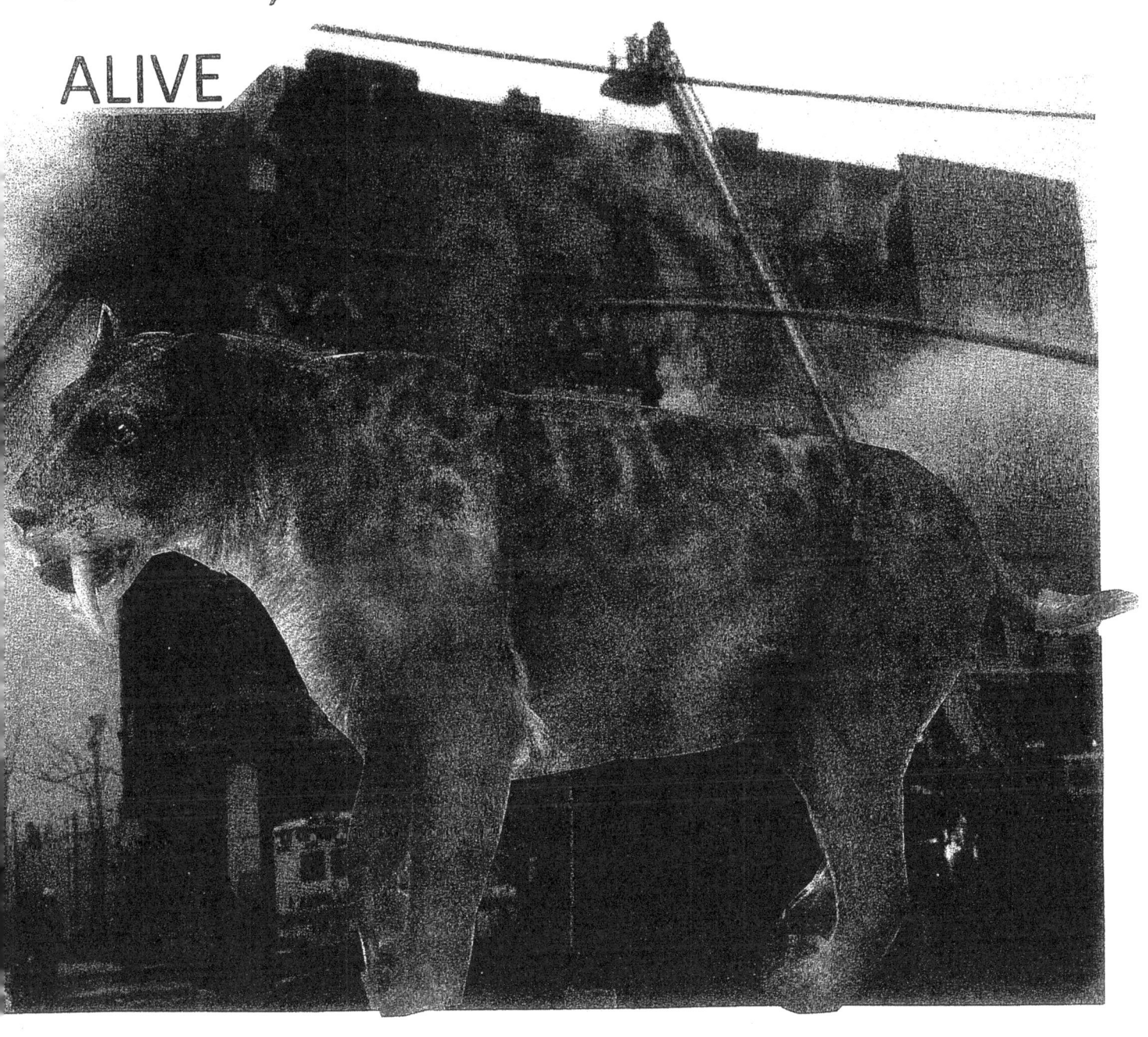

FIREFIGHTERS INCLUDING RETIRED FIREFIGHTER OLD COOT FIGHTING A FIRE IN BROOKLYN

A WALL TOPPLED OVER AND KILLED NEARLY A DOZEN WORKERS IN GREENBELY, MD IN THE 1960s

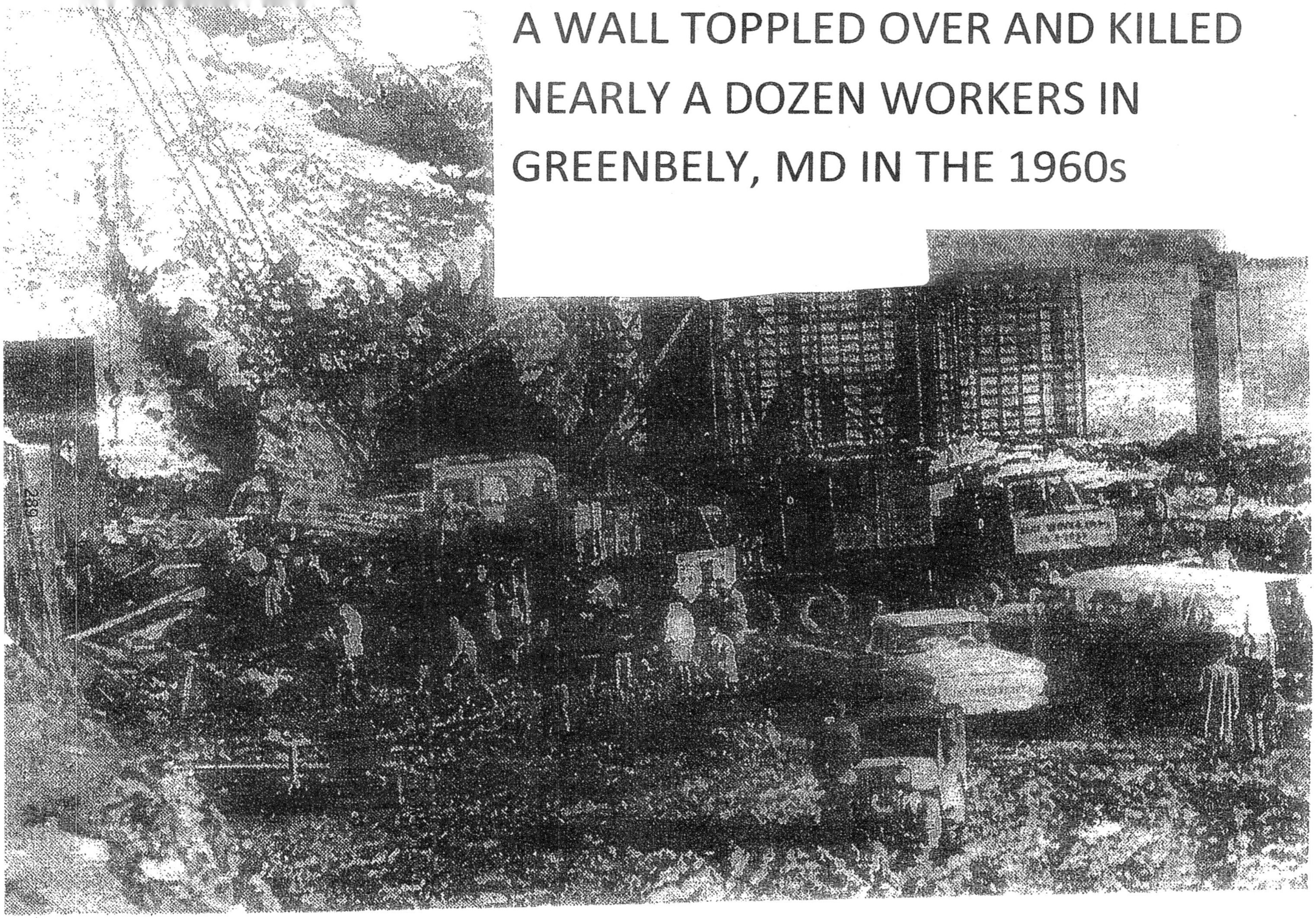

FIRE PREVENTION WEEK AT THE CHEVY CHASE, MD FIRE DEPARTMENT

TRAIN WRECK IN GERMANTOWN

A TIGER IS IN THE PARKING LOT OF A CHURCH SOCIAL HALL THAT BURNED DOWN IN 1956 KILLING AT LEAST 11 VICTIMS WHEN THEY WERE TRAPPED BEHIND A DOOR THAT WOULD NOT OPEN INWARD

KANN'S FIRE

THE DC FIRE CHIEF TOLD US THAT THIS WAS THE WORSE BUILDING FIRE THAT HE HAD SEEN IN HIS OVER 30 YEARS IN THE FIRE SERVICE

A WHITE POLAR BEAR SHOWING HIS STUFF IN FRONT OF A LARGE DEPARTMENT STORE

KANN'S FIRE

A WHITE POLAR BEAR SHOWING HIS STUFF IN FRONT OF A LARGE DEPARTMENT STORE

AT A LARGE FIRE IN THE SOUTH BRONX IN THE 1980s

THIS PET SNAKE NAMED CHARLES RIDES THE FIRE ENGINE AND MOST OF THE TIME ON THE FRONT BUMPER

KANN'S WAREHOUSE IN DC

BURNED DOWN

A 24-HOUR

53

STEVE, AND I ON THE WAY UP TO THE FIRE SAW THE SMOKE AND FLAMES FROM THE NEW JERSEY TURNPIKE

Fatal Oil Fire and Explosion in Newark, NJ

A WAREHOUSE BURNED DOWN IN GAITHERSBURG IN THE 1970s

A DEAD BURNED BODY LIES IN HIS CAR AFTER RUNNING INTO A GASOLINE TANKER TRUCK ON I-95 CAUSING THE CAR TO EXPLODE

BOBBY AND MYSELF AT A FATAL EMPTY CAR CARRIER WRECK AND FIRE ON I-270 SPUR

2 BURNED BODIES STILL IN THE CAB OF THE TRUCK VICTIMS REMAINS BURNED INTO THE TRUCK SEAT SPRINGS

ONE OF THREE FIRE BOATS AT A 5-ALARM FIRE IN THE BRONX

WINSLOW AT A MULTI-ALARM FIRE

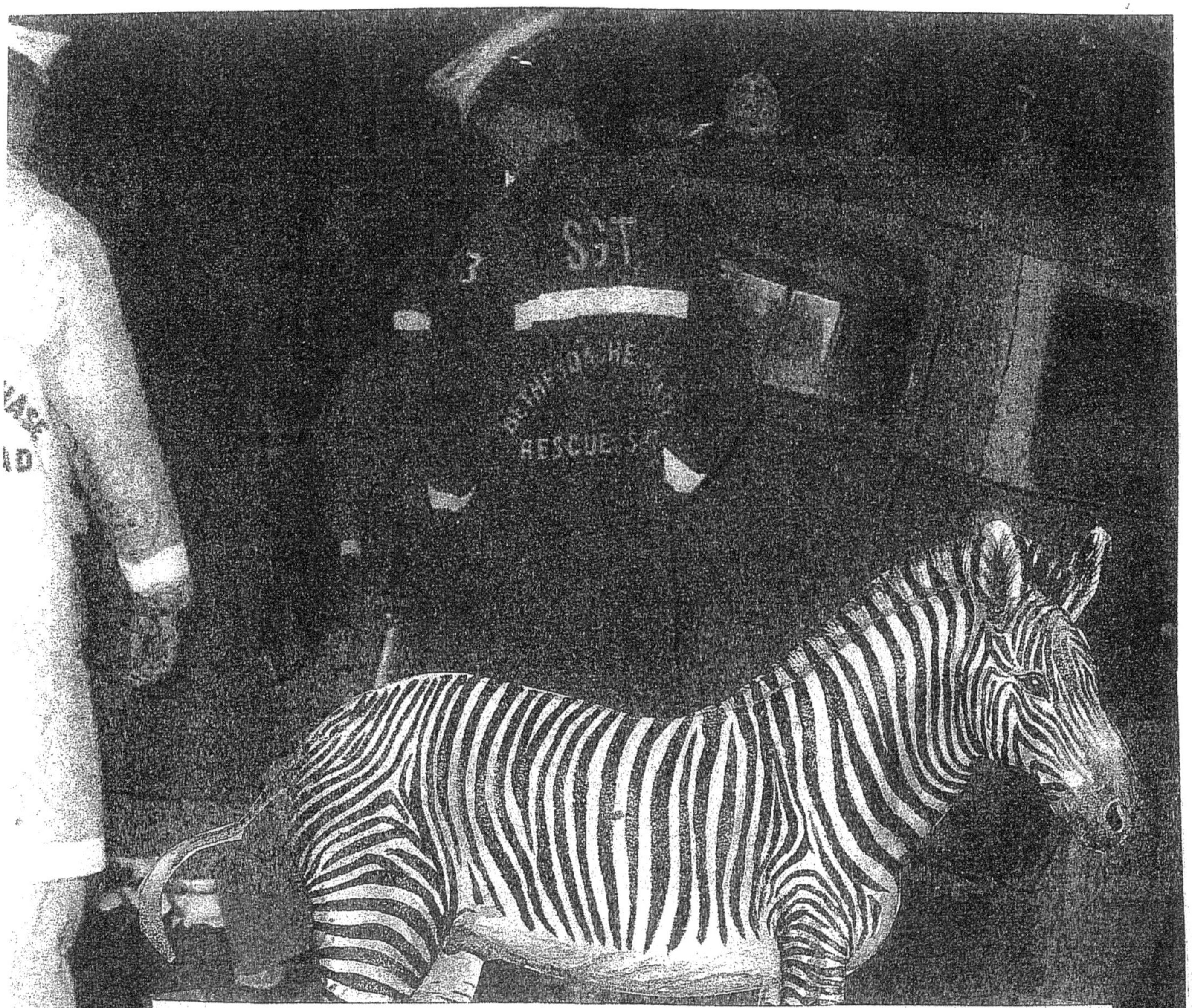

2 SISTERS KILLED WHEN THEY RAN INTO THE REAR OF A DUMP TRUCK IN BETHESDA,

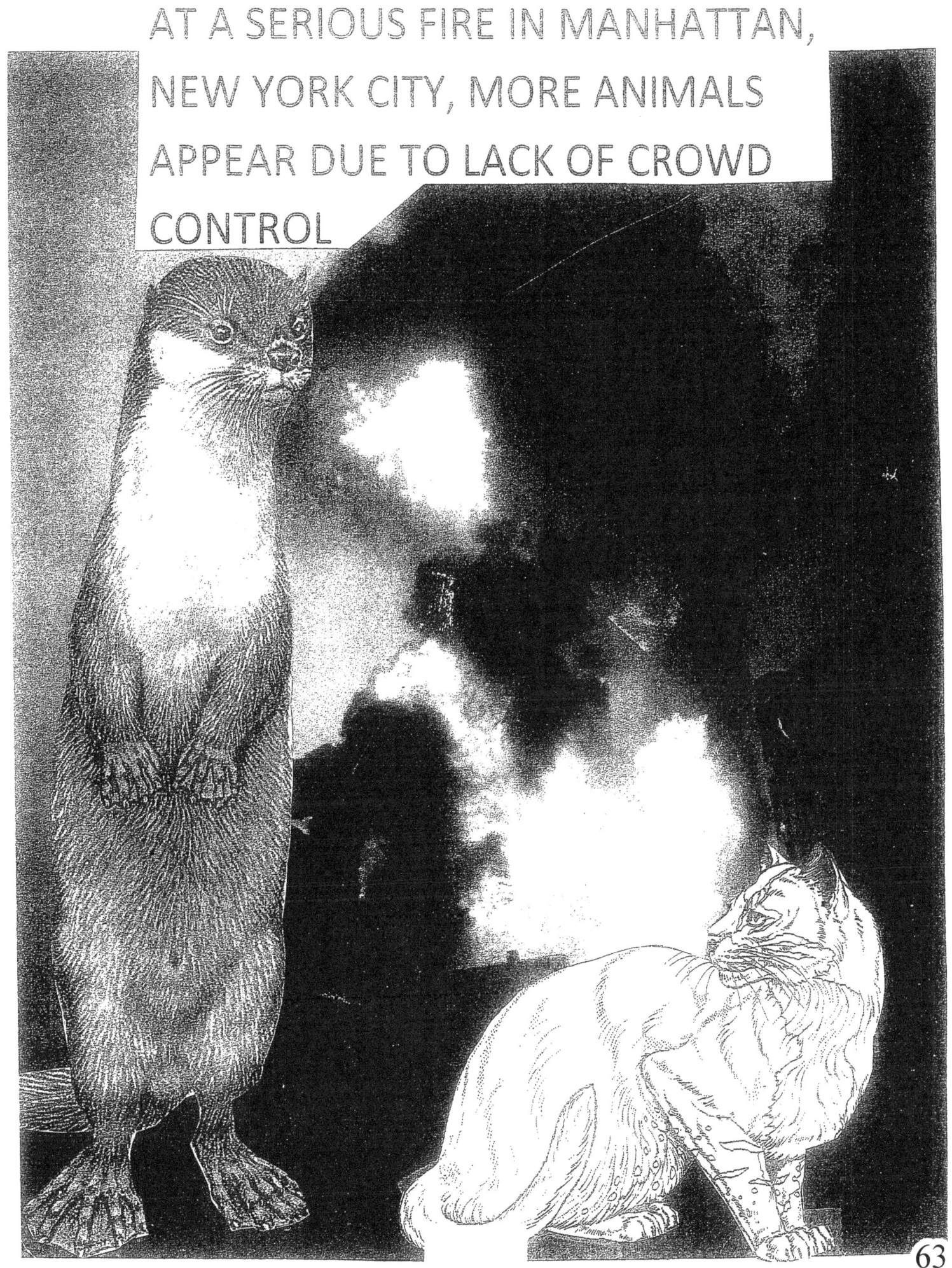

FRIENDLY LION SNIFFING OUT MIZELL LARGE BLAZE

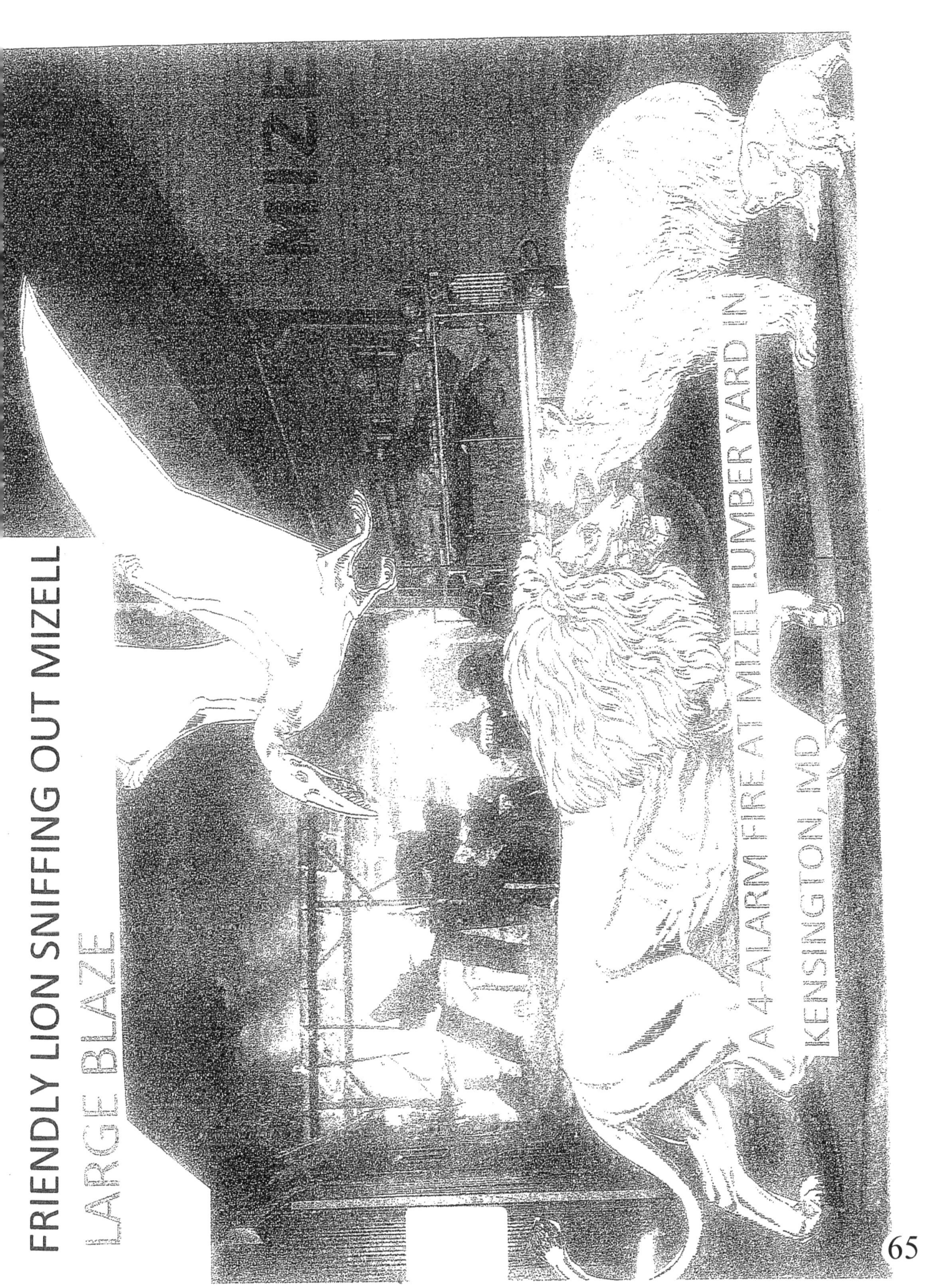

A 4-ALARM FIRE AT MIZEL LUMBER YARD IN KENSINGTON, MD

LARGE FIRE IN THE BRONX

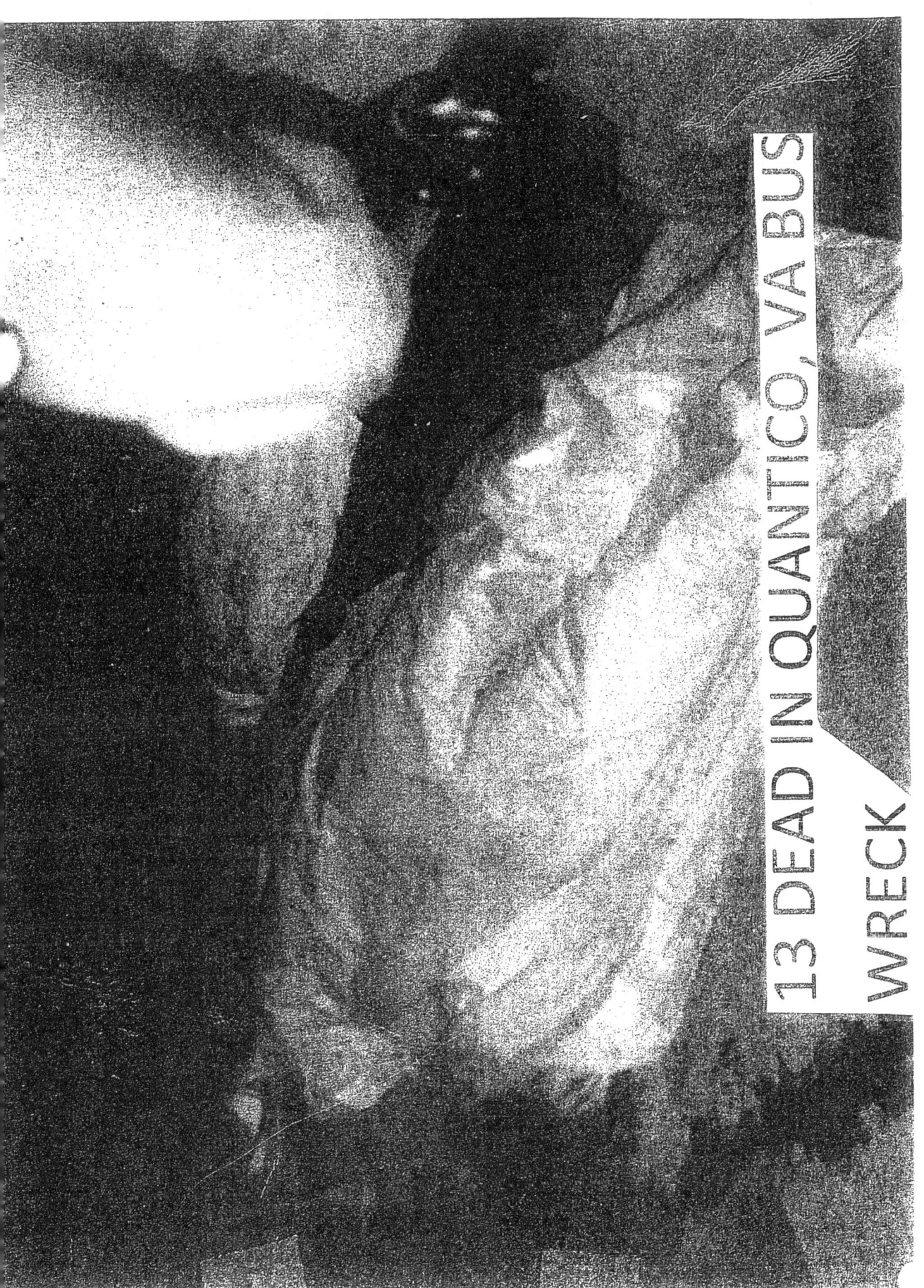

13 DEAD IN QUANTICO, VA BUS WRECK

THIS DUDE FELL SEVERAL HUNDRED FEET AND LANDED ON GRASS BUT STILL WAS KILLED, NOW DAYS THEY HAVE PUT UP FENCE'S ON TOP OF BRIDGE'S TO PREVENT PEOPLE FROM JUMPING TO THEIR DEATH'S

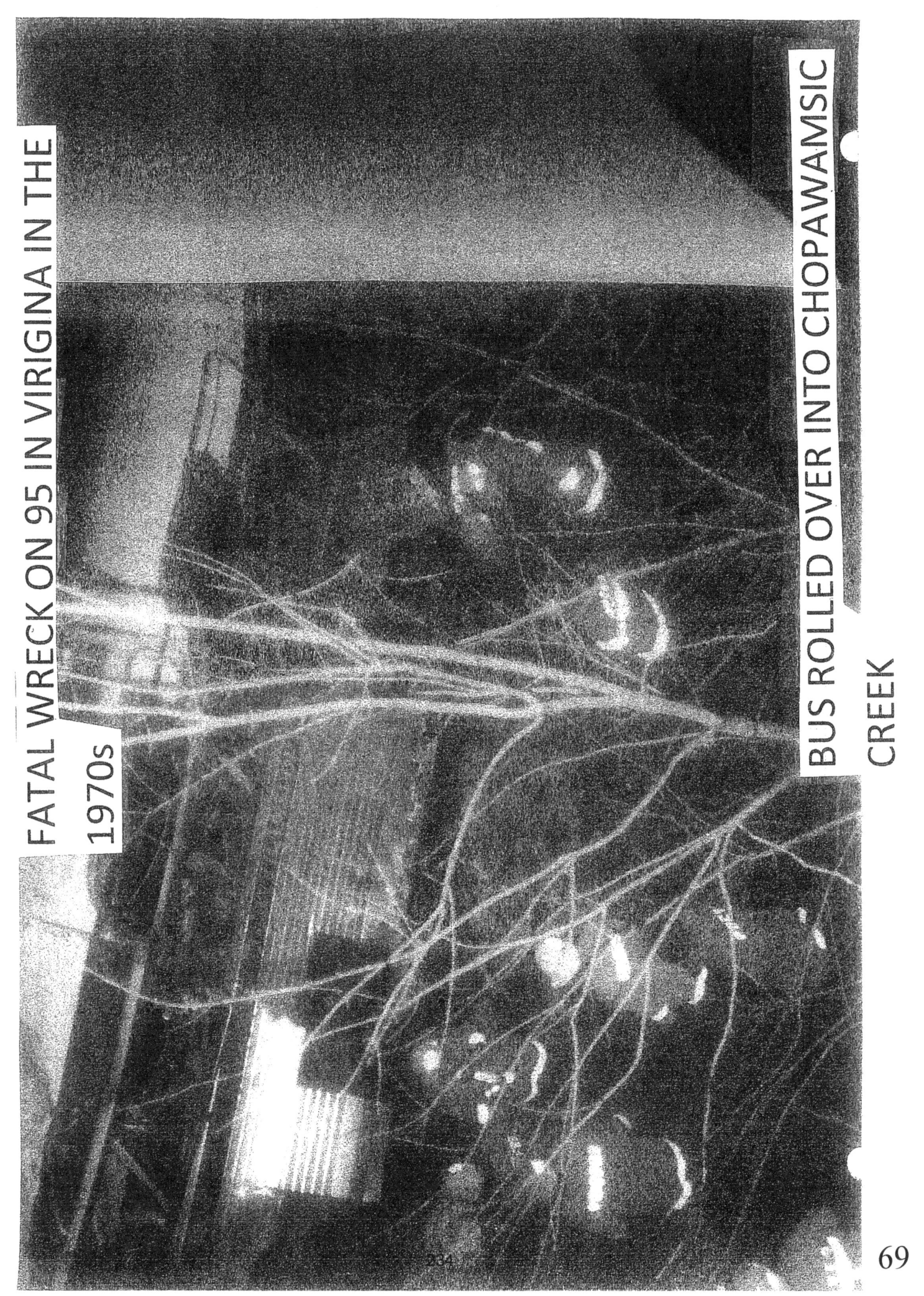

FATAL WRECK ON 95 IN VIRIGINA IN THE 1970s

BUS ROLLED OVER INTO CHOPAWAMSIC CREEK

Recovering Body from Car Near Brighton Dam, MD

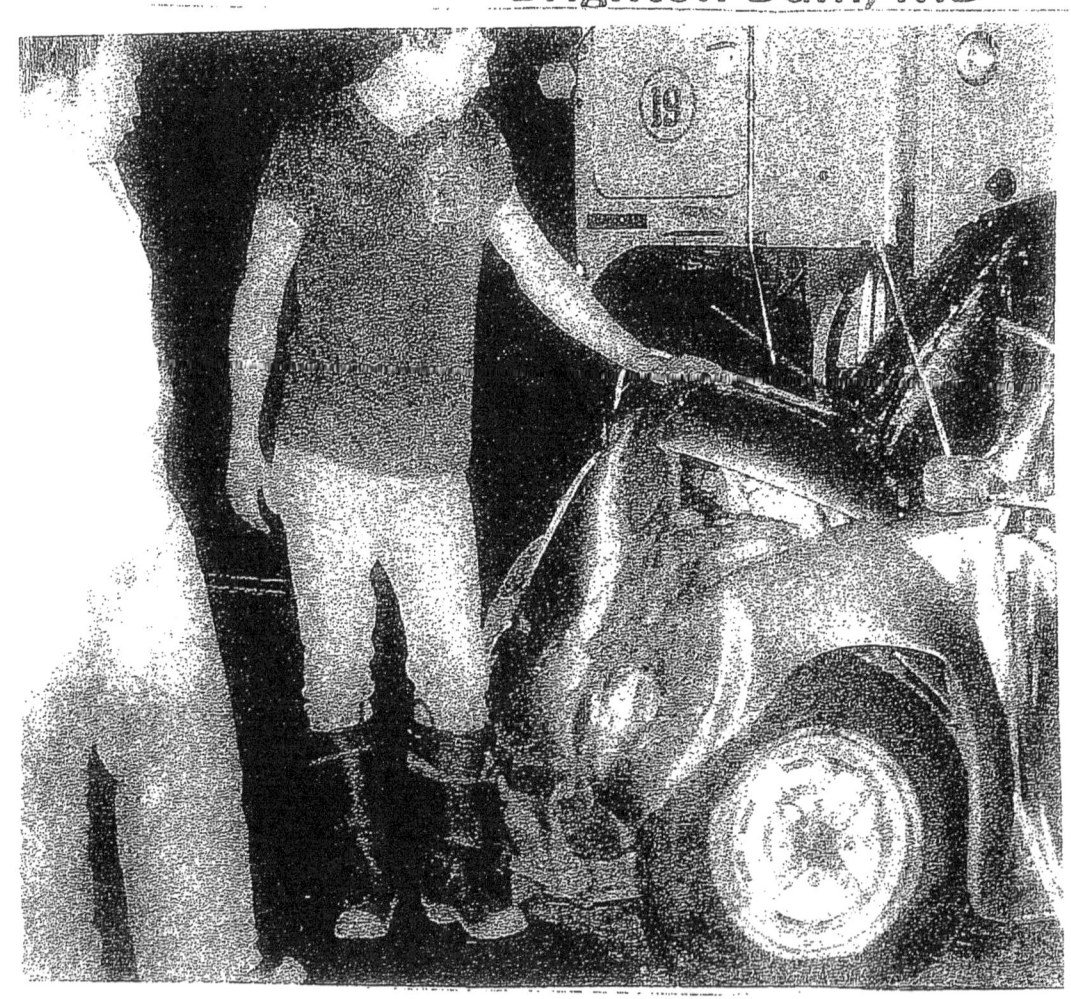

DANNY AND JUNIOR BLACKWOOD AT FATAL ACCIDENT

WENDOVER WILL STATUE WENDOVER NV

Oil Fire in the South Bronx, NY

71

RAISING THE TAIL SECTION OF THE PLANE FROM THE POTOMAC RIVER

PLANE CRASH ON A FARM IN GAITHERSBURG, MD 5 KILLED

5-Alarm Fire RAGES IN Pentagon

THE ONE SPOT DOG NORTH OF SAVAGE MD BURNED DOWN IN THE 1960s IN A 3-ALARM FIRE

A MAJOR FIRE IN THE BRONX, NEW YORK

PLANE CRASH, RICHMOND, VA

77 ARMY RECRUITS KILLED

THE PLANE CRASH IN ELKTON, MD IN A CORNFIELD IN 1963 KILLED 81 PERSONS, FLIGHT 214 A PAN-AMERICAN WORLD AIRWAYS BOEING 707 US

PLANE CRASH NEAR RICHMOND, VIRGINA IN 1961 KILLS 74 ARMY RECRUITS AND 3 PILOTS. A FOUR-ENGINE TRANSPORT
STANDING NEXT TO US WAS A VOL, FIREFIGHTER WHO FROM ALL THE EXCITEMENT CLUTCHED HIS HEART AND FELL DOWN DEAD

THE PLANE CRASH ON TOP OF MOUNT WHEATHER FLIGHT 514 WAS THE LARGEST PLANE CRASH THAT WE WENT ON AT LEAST AS FAR AS THE THE NUMBER OF DEAD AT 92. THE PLANE CAME IN NEAR BERRYVILLE VA. DURING A SEVERE SNOWSTORM IN 1974

THE PLANE WAS A TRANS WORLD AIRLINES BOEING 727

US

PLANE CRASH ON MOUNT WHEATHER

PLANE CRASH CRASH IN ELKTON, MD 81 DEAD

92 DEAD 1974

Jet Crash
Accident Wrecks Homes McLean

McLEAN — Four persons were killed last night in the crash of a twin-engine private jet that exploded over a ...sh neighborhood here, destroying one house and con...lerably damaging a second.

One of the family's two dogs, McGregor, a four-year-old Shetland Sheep dog, was later found by a neighbor, unhurt.

The other dog and the family cat both died in the blaze.

4-Alarm Blaze Fells 36 Firemen

EVERY STORE AND BUILDING ON BOTH SIDES OF THE STREET WERE BURNING OUT OF CONTROL FOR BLOCKS AS FAR AS YOU COULD SEE ON UPPER 14TH STREET WHERE WE WERE OPPERATING AT ON A BUILDING FIRE WITH 2 CHEVY CHASE FIRE ENGINES ON THE SECOND DAY OF THE DC RIOTS

THE D.C. RIOTS

A BODY LYING AT THE BOTTOM OF A 15-FOOT SWIMMING POOL

2 KILLED IN VIRGINIA WRECK

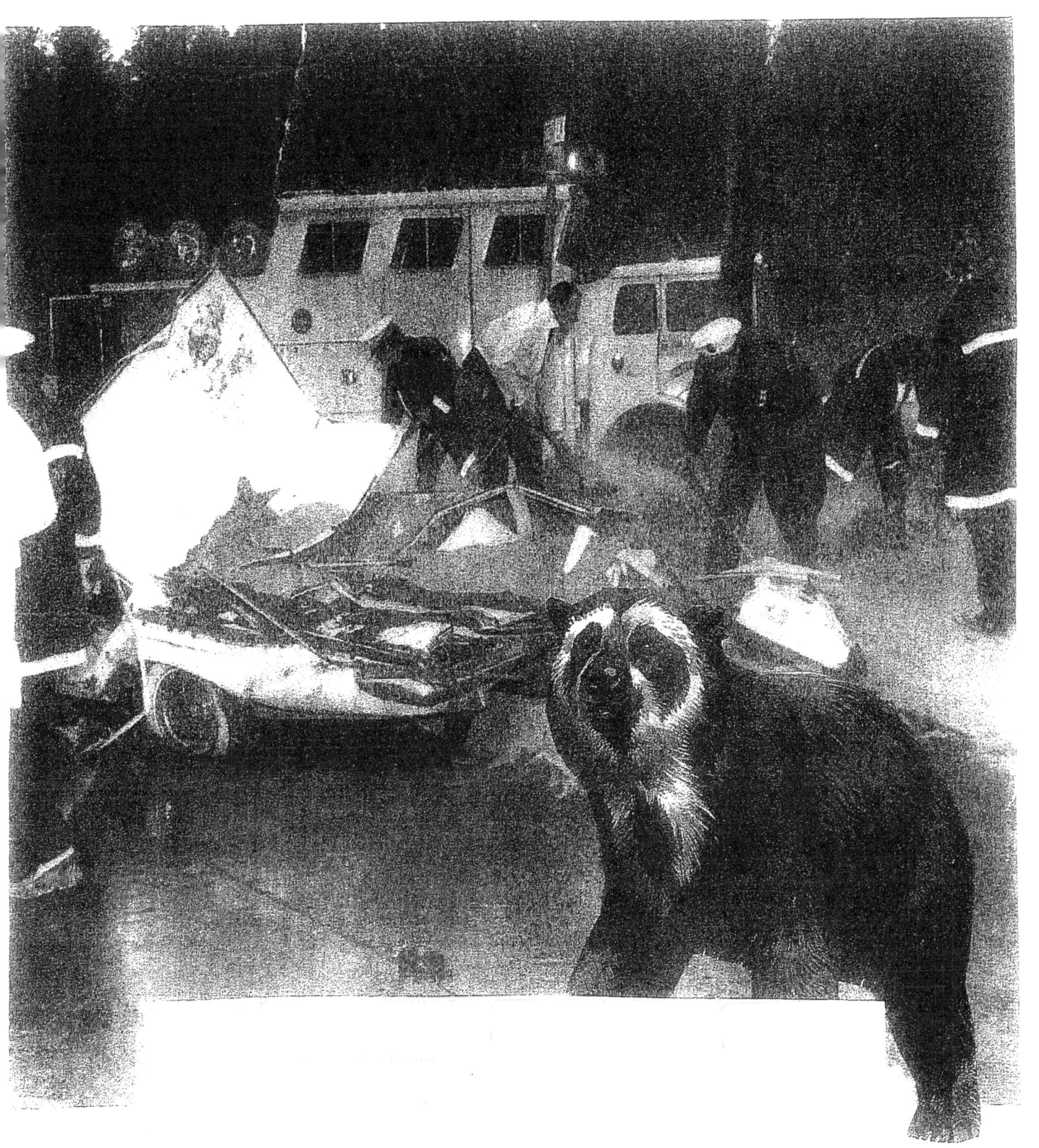

WOMAN KILLED WHEN A TRACTOR TRAILER OVERTURNED ON HER CAR

NOTE DO YOU SEE THE CHARED SKULL SITTING IN THE DOORWAY OF THE BURNED UP VAN

IT IS ALMOST LIKE SATAN HAD A HAND IN BINDING AND KILLING AND BURNING THESE 2 DRUG DEALERS IN THEIR FULLY ENVOLVED VAN IN UPPER MARLBORO IN THE 1970s

THE 2 DUDES BOTH DRUG DEALERS WERE FOUND IN THIS BURNING VAN, BOTH WITH THE HANDS HANDCUFFED BEHIND THEIR BACKS AND SHOT IN THE HEAD

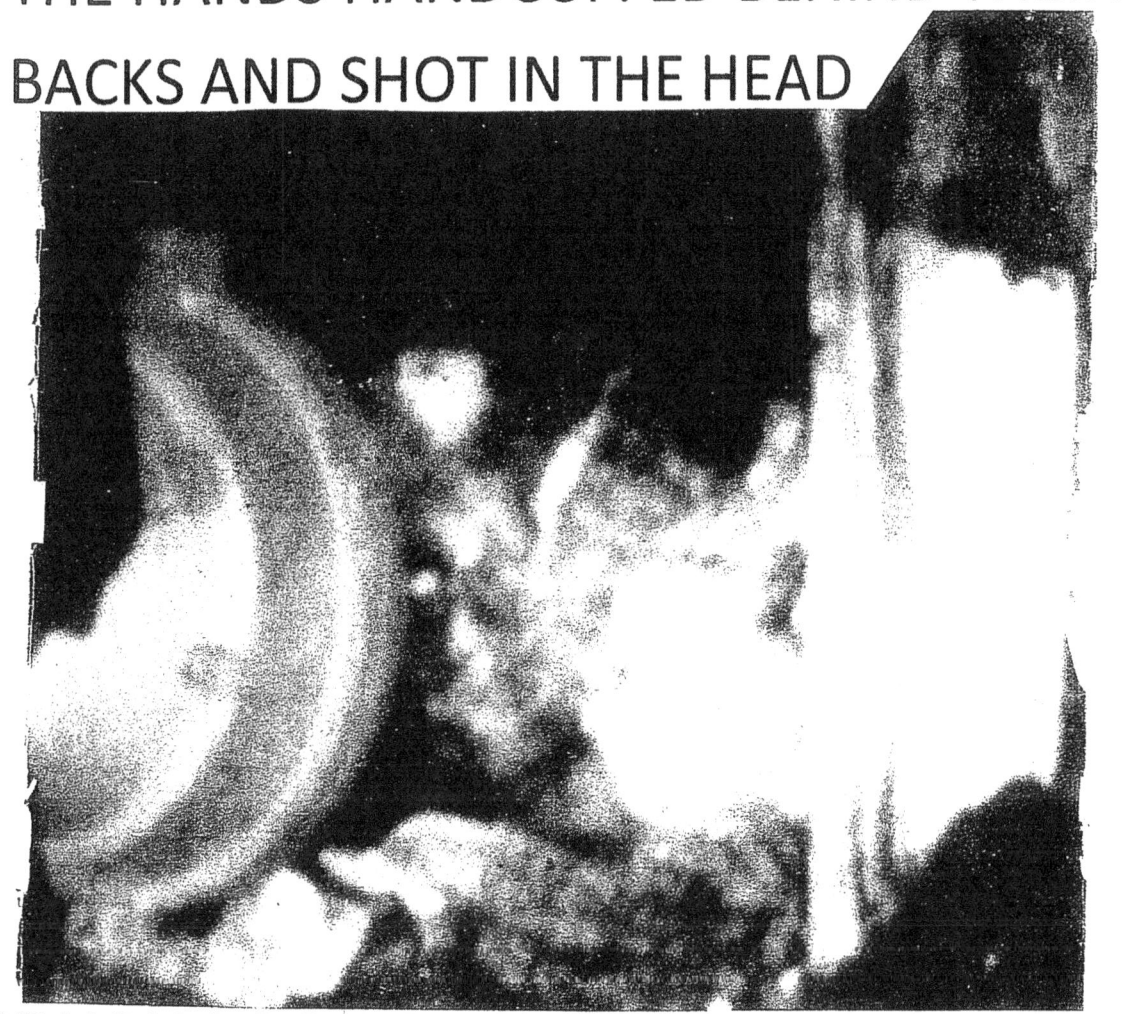

IF YOU LOOK CAREFULLY YOU CAN SEE THE OUTLINE OF ONE OF THE SKULLS THAT APPEARS TO BE LOOKING AT YOU

OVERTURNED LUMBER TRUCK IN KENSINGTON, MD KILLING 3 PERSONS WAITING AT A BUS STOP

TONY VEITH AND MYSELF WENT UP TO OWENS MILLS, MD FOR A MULTI-ALARM OLD WHISKY BREWERY THAT BURNED DOWN ONE NIGHT

Small Plane Crash at Private Airport in Frederick County – 1 Fatality

Silver Spring Bakery Burns, 9 Are Injured

Loss Estimated At $300,000 in Wind-Whipped Fire

Nine persons were injured in a fire yesterday which destroyed the interior of Mrs. Smith's Colonial Baking Co. on Colonial lane just off Georgia avenue in Silver Spring.

More than 200 firemen from nine engine companies fought the wind-whipped flames for about six hours at the two-story quonset hut.

Allan Fausak, manager of the bakery, estimated the value of the building and equipment at $500,000.

Mr. Fausak said the firm, which employed 105 persons, would begin making plans immediately for a new bakery.

Other Mrs. Smith's bakery plants are in Philadelphia, York and Morgantown, Pa., with headquarters in Pottstown, Pa.

BATTLING BAKERY BLAZE—More than 200 firemen fought six hours to control a general alarm fire at the Colonial Baking Co. in Silver Spring yesterday. Nine persons were released from Washington Sanitarium after emergency treatment they required from fighting the $300,000 fire.—Photo by Bill Glascock.

NEARLY A DOZEN WORKERS ARE KILLED IN A CONSTRUCTION INCIDENT IN GREENBELT, MD

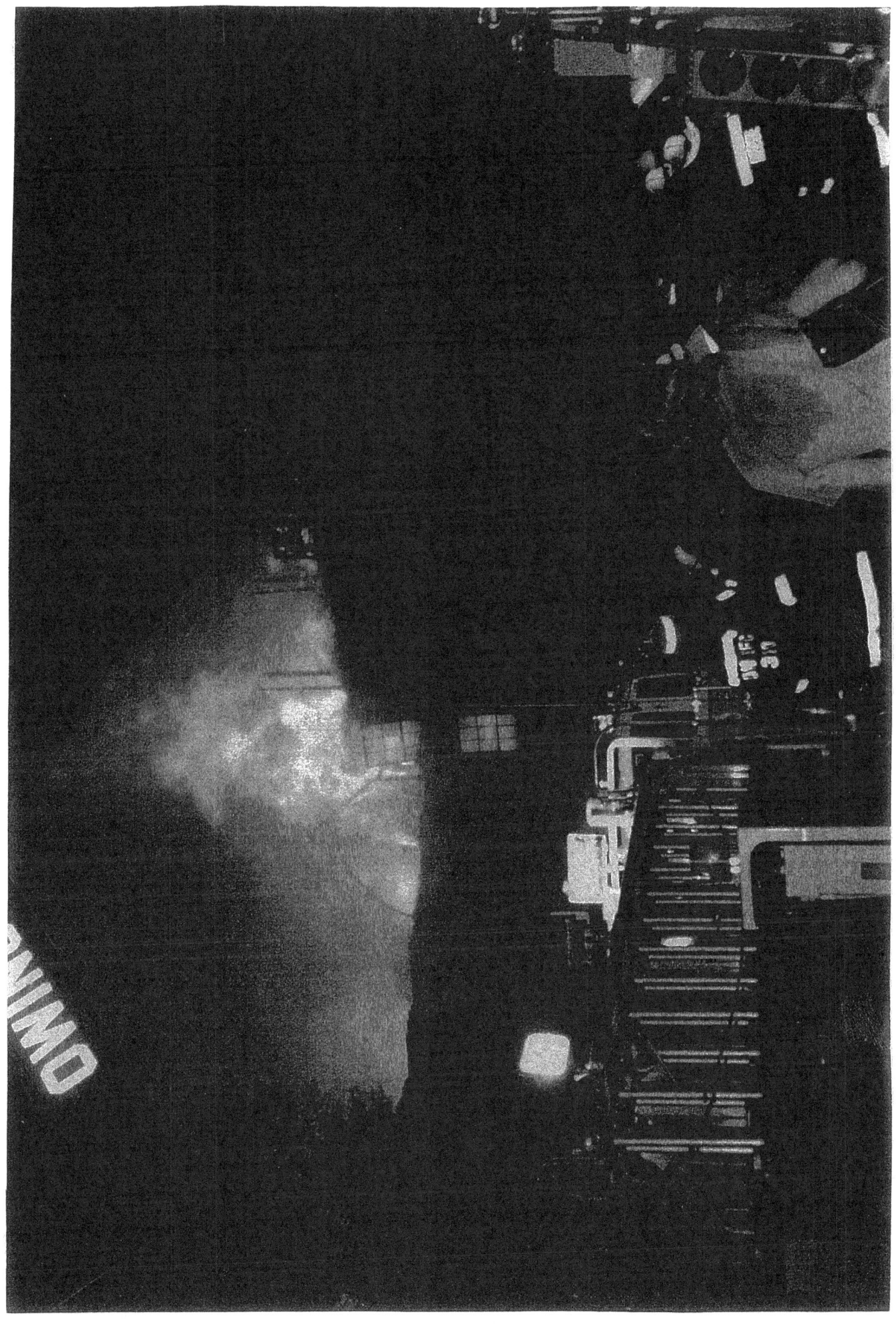

TANKER TRUCKS OVERTURNED IN CHEMICAL EXPLOSION IN NEWARK, NJ

TRAIN FIRE THREATENS HOMES

Six tank cars carrying petroleum burst into flames at 5:30 a.m. yesterday when 41 cars of a 110-car Pennsylvania Railroad train jumped the tracks just west of Elkton, Md.

La Plata tower gone, may not be rebuilt

The deadly F4-class tornado that ripped through Southern Maryland last month did some of its heaviest damage in downtown La Plata, the Charles County seat. One of the tornado's casualties was the 75,000-gallon water tower, a town landmark since it was built in 1927.

La Plata mayor Bill Eckman says the water tower may not be rebuilt. "The tower was completely destroyed," Mr. Eckman says. "The only question will be whether we rebuild the tower or not."

Fortunately for La Plata, the tower was not the town's only one. Mr. Eckman says three other towers have been built in La Plata since 1927, bringing the total storage capability to 1.2 million gallons. Because of that, the water tower that was destroyed provided an "insignificant amount of storage" for the growing county seat.

"At the time this town was built, La Plata had only 1,200 acres," Mr. Eckman says. "Now we have 5,500 acres. We needed more towers. The system is much wider now."

Mr. Eckman says city officials will run some computer models to determine whether a rebuilt tower will be needed, but he says it probably won't be.

"We'd obviously prefer not to build it back if we don't have to," Mr. Eckman says. "It probably will cost around $300,000 to do it, and that's $300,000 we could spend in plenty of other ways with the damage we've had."

— Mark Stewart

Members of an Amish community were dwarfed by the wreckage of a water tower in La Plata, Md., when they walked past it April 29, the day after the tower and much of the town were destroyed by a tornado.
Photo by Rod A. Lamkey Jr./The Washington Times

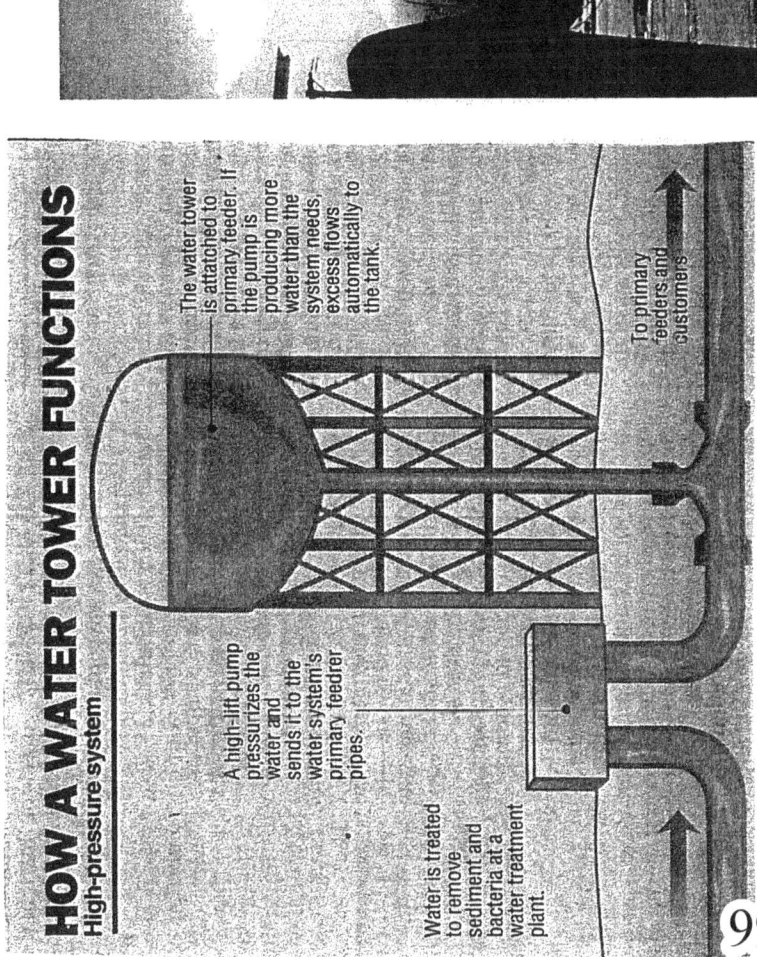

HOW A WATER TOWER FUNCTIONS
High-pressure system

Water is treated to remove sediment and bacteria at a water treatment plant.

A high-lift pump pressurizes the water and sends it to the water system's primary feeder pipes.

The water tower is attached to primary feeder. If the pump is producing more water than the system needs, excess flows automatically to the tank.

To primary feeders and customers

99

A WHOLE CITY-BLOCK BURNED IN BALTIMORE, MD IN THE 1980s

PRINCE, THE BCCRS MASCOT, IN 1956

THE GOODWILL INDUSTRIES IN WESTMISTER, MD BURNED DOWN ONE NIGHT IN THE 1980s

TRAIN HIT A LUMBER TRUCK IN BETHESDA, MD

By FREDERICK A. MCCORD

A LITTLE BOY sat between two men in a horse and buggy, jogging east on Washington Lane, across Chew Street in Germantown. He was, the men had told him, on his way to their Aunt Susie's candy store.

It was four in the afternoon that July 1, 1874. The little boy was Charles Brewster Ross, whose well-to-do parents had given him a fourth birthday party two months before.

His home, a big stone mansion on Washington Lane surrounded by spacious grounds, was disappearing behind the buggy. The two men were carrying Charlie off in what was to be the first sensational kidnapping of modern times.

No one who knew him was ever to see Charlie Ross again. The mystery of his fate fascinated generations of Americans and made his name one which conjured up great dread in households throughout the nation during the secure and comfortable years up to and past the turn of the century.

But as the horse trotted over Washington Lane towards Limekiln Pike, Charlie Ross was just a trusting little boy looking forward to the visit to Aunt Susie's candy store.

He presumably felt no fear of the two men because on several occasions during the previous week they had stopped at the mansion's gateway, talked in a friendly way with him and his brother, Walter, six, given candy to them,

In addition, Walter, the big brother, was sitting along on the side. Walter sat beside Charlie on the lap of one of the men. He alone was to come home from the trip, but it was carrying Charlie into oblivion.

Walter was a precocious child, and when he returned to tell about the buggy ride and the two men was to feed a half-century of speculation on what happened to Charlie Ross.

The day of the kidnapping was warm and sunny, but not uncomfortably so. What was then called the Great and Glorious Fourth was only three days away. Charlie's excitement over its approach was at a fever in the tragedy.

The little boys' mother was ailing and had gone to Atlantic City to rest. Other children in the family were visiting relatives. Charlie and Walter were at home with the servants and their father, Christian K. Ross, a prosperous jeweler.

The father had promised his sons a big sandpile on the lawn as part of their Fourth of July party. He closed his store early and was buying the sand, arranging to have it carted home, when Charlie and Walter, who had strayed from the mansion's grounds, looked up Washington Lane and saw the two men in the familiar buggy approaching.

The two men hoisted the brothers candy, Charlie began talking about firecrackers for the Fourth and Walter said he knew of a store where they could get some. The men said they knew of a better store. It was run by their Aunt Susie and ch… was a whole pocketful of crackers for a nickel. They helped Charlie and Walter into the buggy. The driver flicked the reins and they went off.

It was a long ride, and circuitous (Walter was later to retrace it street by street), and as it went on and on the friendly men grew silent. Charlie began to cry and said he wanted to go home. They petted him and soothed him with more candy.

The buggy turned southeast on Limekiln Pike and descended into what is now Oak Lane, then Frankford, Kensington, finally Fishtown. At Palmer and Richmond streets the driver pulled up. The man holding Walter gave him a quarter, pointed to a store near the corner and said that was Aunt Susie's.

Walter was to buy firecrackers for himself and Charlie. He scrambled out of the buggy, trotted over to the store, bought two packs of firecrackers and a package of torpedoes, got four pennies in change and hurried back to the street. The buggy and Charlie were gone. Walter began to cry. A crowd gathered, and

Continued

Only a Dead Man Knew Where the Boy Was

by an odd coincidence it included a man named Peacock who knew the Ross family, recognized Walter, and took him home.

The father, meanwhile, with mounting apprehension had been searching for his sons through the fields and copses that then made up much of the neighborhood. When Walter was brought home and he heard the story from its beginning he sent an immediate telegram to Philadelphia police, asking them if anyone had brought them his son.

Germantown was then a remote suburb and Alexander Graham Bell was still two years away from speaking the first words over a telephone.

The search went on, but the lines of communication were slow in an era when prowl cars and their minute-by-minute calls were undreamed of.

A day-and-night watch was put on ferries, railroads and bridges. Vessels on the two rivers, empty barns and houses and covered vehicles moving through the city were searched. House-to-house hunts were made in neighborhoods considered likely to harbor the kidnappers.

One of the father's concerns was to keep the fearful news from his ailing wife. For a week he managed to do so.

He advertised to the kidnappers in the newspapers, not naming his son and covering his own identity by using an intermediary.

In the ads, E. L. Joyce, Central Station, corner of 5th and Chestnut Streets, offered a suitable reward for the return of "a small boy, four years old, having long, curly, flaxen hair, hazel eyes, clear, light skin and round face, dressed in a brown linen suit, with a short-brimmed hat and laced shoes."

And when Mrs. Ross could no longer be protected, tens of thousands of circulars bearing her ringleted little boy's picture were spread throughout the United States.

They bore the headline, "Abduction of Charlie Brewster Ross". The word "kidnapping," while it had come into the language in the late 17th Century to describe the carrying off of boys and girls for servitude in England's overseas possessions, was not in common usage and its meaning was not then generally understood.

The circulars gave many clues on how to recognize Charlie. He could recite: "Jesus loves me, this I know, for the Bible tells me so." He could recognize "o" and "s" but not the other letters of the alphabet. He gave his name as Charlie Ross and, if asked if he had another name, would answer, "Charlie Brewster Ross."

And with the real Charlie Ross it would be possible to hold a colloquy as follows:

Q. Who is your uncle in Washington Lane?
A. Uncle Joe.

Q. What is your cousin's name?
A. Cousin Joe or Cousin George or Cousin Frank.
Q. Who lives next door to Papa?
A. Marcellus McDowell or Jennie McDowell.
Q. What horse does Mamma ride?
A. Polly.

Ross's first response from the kidnappers came three days after the abduction. He then received an illiterate letter which had been mailed in Philadelphia. It said:

"Mr. Ros: be not uneasy you son Charley bruster be all writ we is got him and no powers on earth can deliver out our hand, you will have two pay us befor you git him..."

A few days later there was another letter, demanding $20,000 ransom. Ross and his friends raised the money. The father advertised his readiness to deliver it.

Then Mayor William Stokley offered a $20,000 reward for the recovery of the boy and conviction of the kidnappers. Communications from the criminals stopped for a week but finally resumed with the kidnappers rebuking Ross for having confided in the authorities.

At last they sent him a letter from New York giving explicit directions for payment of the ransom. The father followed them, carrying a bag containing $20,000. He rode the back platform of trains between Philadelphia and New York, and New York and Albany, looking for the signal to drop the bag to the tracks. It was to be given him by a man with a white flag and a torch. Ross never got it.

There followed more exchanges with the kidnappers. They led nowhere. Meanwhile, New York police stepped into the case when Chief George Walling was visited by a man who said that two men calling themselves Johnson and Clark had approached him with the idea of abducting one of the Vanderbilt children at Throg's Neck, Long Island.

Walling established that Johnson and Clark were really William Mosher and Joseph Douglass, who had criminal records as burglars and river pirates up and down the east coast. He remembered that when last seen the buggy had been carrying Charlie towards the Delaware. Could it have been towards a small craft used by the river pirates?

Walling's men couldn't find the hunted pair. But Mosher's brother-in-law was William A. Westervelt, who had been dismissed from the New York police force a short time before. Walling called Westervelt in, offered him reinstatement on the force and $20,000 reward for the return of Charlie Ross. Westervelt agreed to try.

On December 14, 1874, five months after the kidnapping, at 2 A.M. in the Bay Ridge section of Brooklyn, a householder named J. Holmes Van Brunt was awakened by a ringing burglar alarm in the nearby unoccupied home of his brother.

Van Brunt and his son, Albert, armed themselves with shotguns, surprised two men leaving the house and shot them down. One of them was killed, the other mortally wounded.

"Men," he said, "I won't lie to you. My name is Joseph Douglass and that man is William Mosher. We stole Charlie Ross in Germantown."

Where was the boy? Douglass didn't know. It was the dead Mosher's secret. But, said Douglass, Charlie was safe and could be found. Two hours later Douglass died.

Walter Ross was taken to New York. He looked at the bodies and said they were those of the men in the buggy. Mosher, he said, was the one who held him on his lap.

THE IDENTIFICATION and Douglass' assertion that Charlie was safe were to be the mainstay of those who in the years to follow were to argue that Charlie Ross still lived, had not been killed by his kidnappers.

The suspicion arose that Westervelt, far from collaborating in the hunt for Charlie, had really been keeping Mosher and Douglass informed of police moves. He was indicted, convicted in Philadelphia and sentenced to seven years imprisonment. In April, 1882, he was released and then disappeared as completely as Charlie Ross.

Charlie's father never gave up hope. He spent $60,000 on 200 journeys to run down clues to the fate of his son. All were false. He and his wife looked at 270 children offered to them as Charlie, and each time reluctantly concluded that here was not their son.

The father, heartbroken, his fortune depleted, died in 1897; the mother in 1912. In the years that followed there was a steady procession of men presenting themselves as Charlie Ross.

They included a Bowery derelict who was vaccinated—and so was Charlie; a West Virginia farmer who remembered a long and mysterious train ride as a boy; a North Carolina mountaineer, who remembered a boyhood trip with an itinerant peddler; a Phoenix, Arizona, carpenter who recalled boyhood years spent in a cave, and a hermit in Croydon who posted his shack with the sign: "This place is wired with dynamite. Be careful."

With his father's death Walter Ross examined all these claims, found none of them valid. He became a successful stockbroker and died July 22, 1943, at the age of 74.

The Ross mansion was torn down in 1926. Its grounds are now the site of the Cliveden Presbyterian Church. ∎

--Star Photographer Ken Heinen

An early train stops alongside the burned-out B&O station house in Takoma Park after this morning's multi-alarm fire.

Historic Train Station Burns in Takoma Park

By WALTER GOLD
Star Staff Writer

A spectacular multi-alarm fire early today destroyed the landmark Takoma Park B&O railroad station at Blair Road and Carroll Avenue NW.

Shortly after 4 a.m., flames consumed the two-story wooden former station house, which currently was being used as a warehouse by a local home construction firm.

Nearly 100 members of the District Fire Department fought the blaze for about half an hour before bringing it under control. All that was left at the end was a burned out shell of a once-busy passenger and freight station.

Origin Unknown

Although the B&O quit using the structure years ago, the railroad still retained title to the land and to the building. Daily commuter trains still stop outside the station house, which had been slated for preservation for its old architecture.

It may be impossible to tell what started the blaze, fire officials said today as they continued their investigation. An estimated $7,000 worth of home building material, including lumber, which was stored inside the old station house also was destroyed by the fire.

A passer-by who discovered flames coming from the wooden landmark about 4:16 a.m. pulled the first fire box alarm. The normally busy intersection, located only a few blocks from Takoma Park, Md., was cleared of light traffic and spectators as firemen arrived and went to work to save the station.

Built in Mid-1800s

The station house, built in the late 1800s, was being leased by Pre-Fab, Inc., the home building firm. B&O officials could not immediately estimate the value of the station house, they said.

Several B&O trains were briefly delayed but by rush-hour, commuters were standing on the station's platform amid tangled fire hose, waiting for their trains.

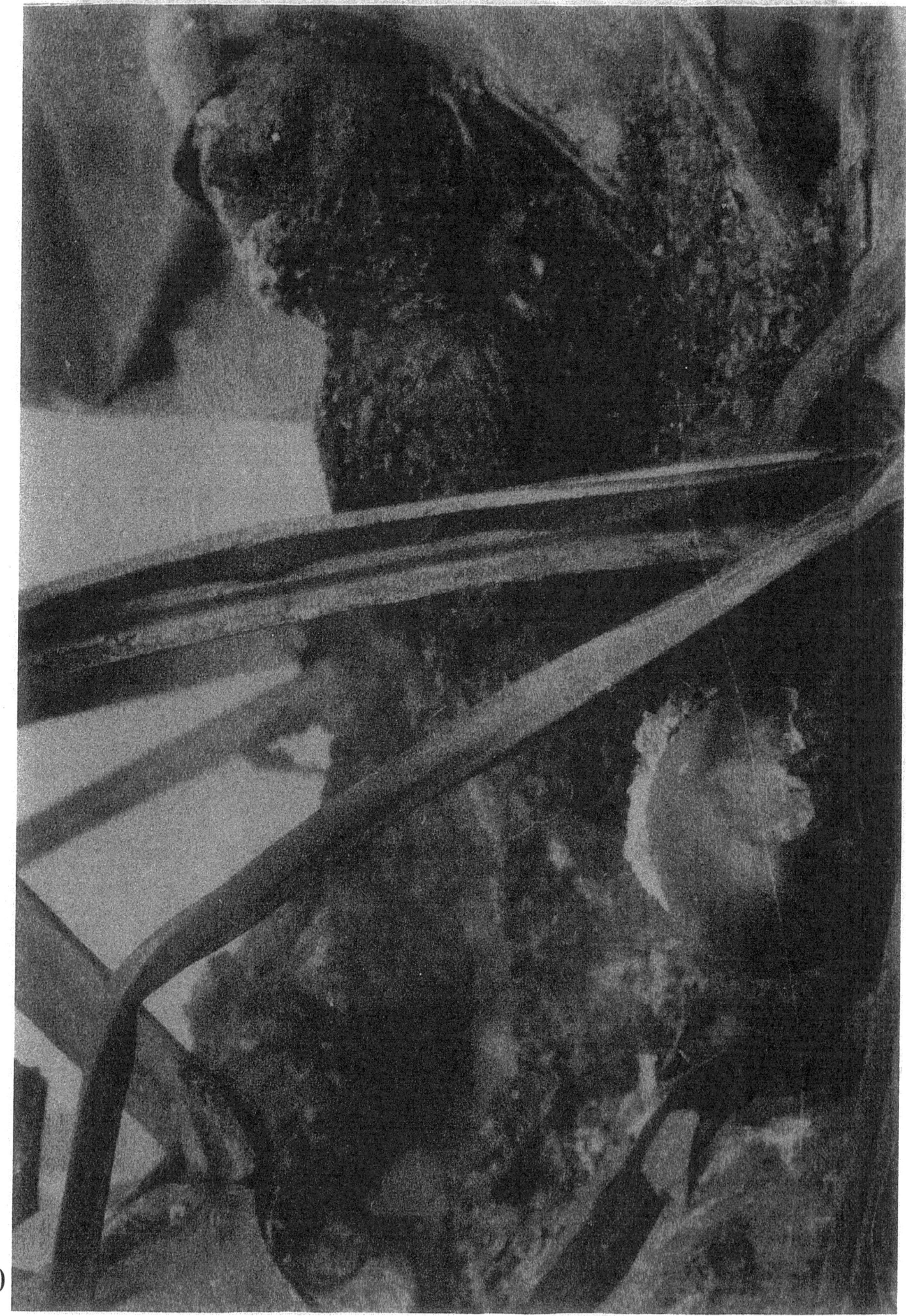

4-ALARM FIRE IN GERMANTOWN, MD

FIREFIGHTERS AFTER PUTTING OUT A FIRE IN A GAS STATION

A FRIENDLY LION VISITING THE SUPER PUMPER JUST BEFORE BEING RETIRED FROM THE FIRE SERVICE IN THE 1980s

FATAL WRECK FIREFIGHTERS TRYING TO REMOVE THE DRIVER OF THIS OVERTURNED PICKUP TRUCK

A 3 OR 4-ALARM FIRE AT THE NORGE LAUNDRY IN WHEATON, MD

A CHIEF OFFICER FROM THE BCCRS AT THE GENERAL ALARM OIL FIRE IN BETHESDA, MD IN NOVEMBER 1958

A 4-ALARM FIRE IN KENSINGTON AT A LUMBERYARD

PLANE CRASH INTO THE POTOMAC RIVER IN THE 1970s

ROW OF SOME OLD BUILDINGS AND A MOVIE THEATRE BURNED IN BETHESDA MD ONE AFTERNOON IN A HUGE FIRE

THE WASHINGTONIAN MOTEL BURNS DOWN IN A 4-ALARM FIRE IN GAITHERSBURG, MD

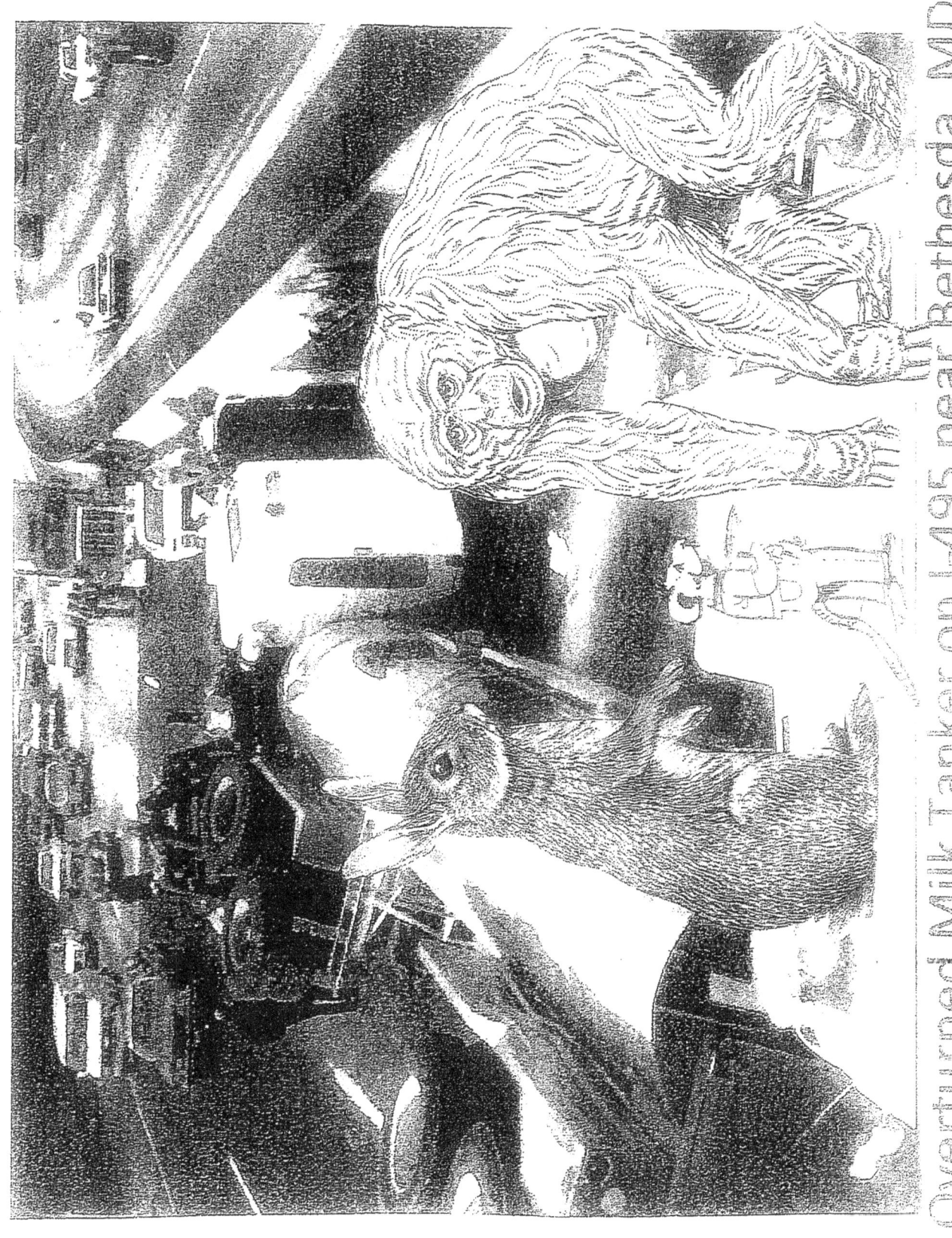
Overturned Milk Tanker on I-495 near Bethesda, MD

FIREFIGHTER ED DROOL THE 2ND TAKING IN NIAGARA FALLS

NIAGARA FALLS, YEARS AGO THE ELDERLY BUCK WENT OVER THE AMERICAN FALLS IN AN ICE CHEST AND DIDN'T GIVE A DAM

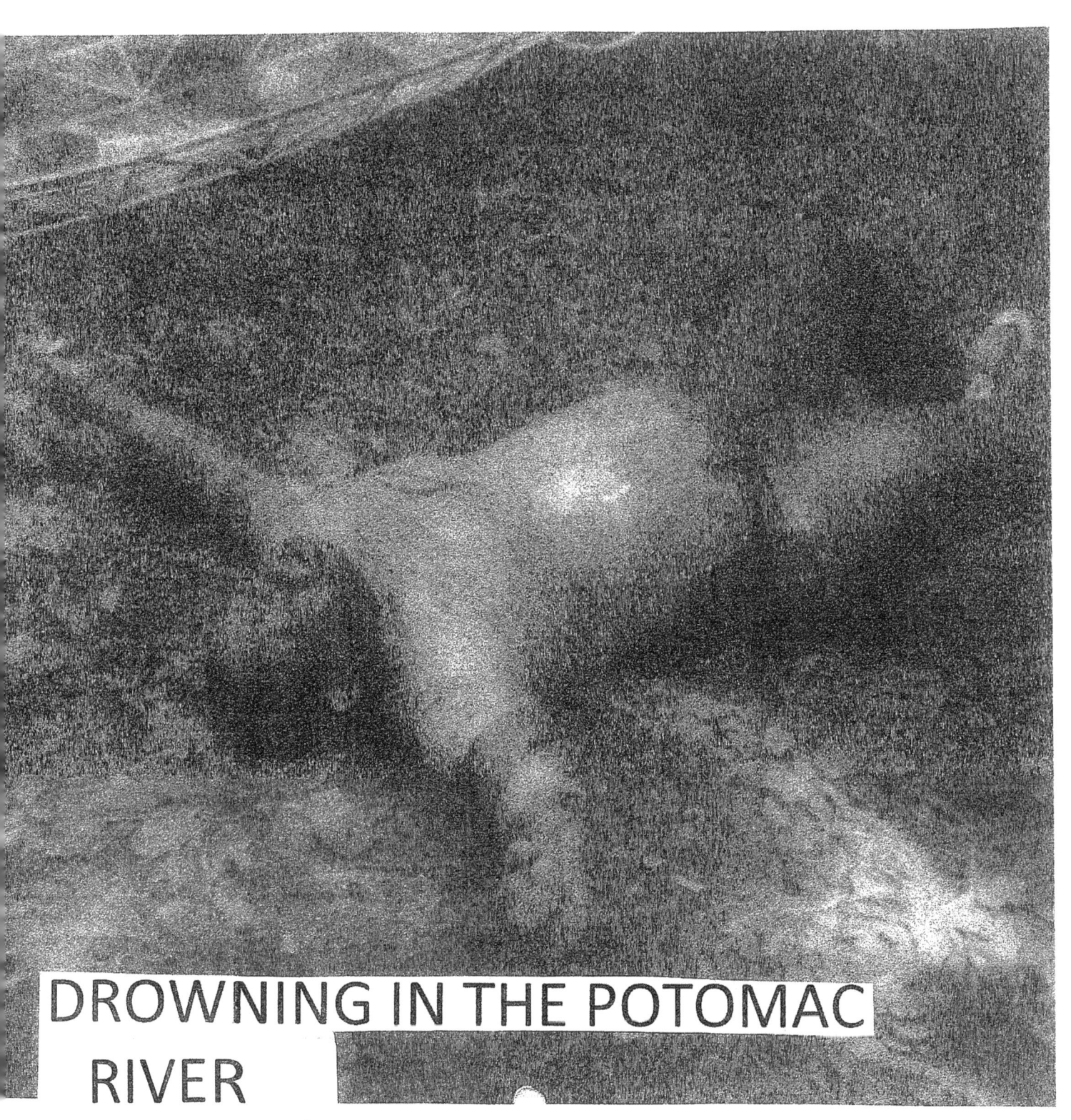

DROWNING IN THE POTOMAC RIVER

A BURNING BUILDING IN THE TOWN OF WESTMINSTER, MARYLAND

IF ANY OF THIS BOTHERS YOU THEN JUST DON'T READ OR LOOK AT IT

MONK

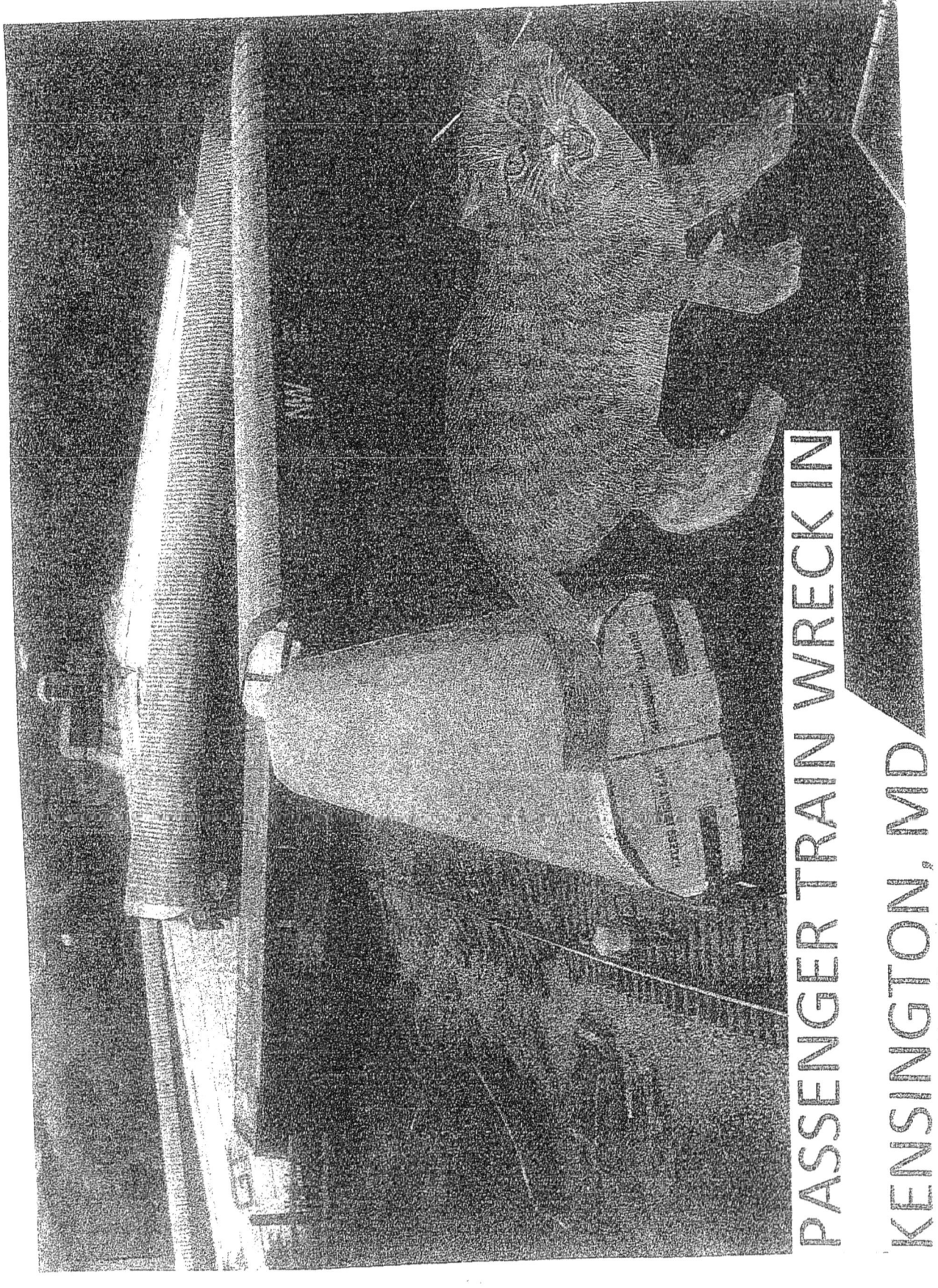

PASSENGER TRAIN WRECK IN KENSINGTON, MD

ANIMALS WANDERING AROUND THE STREETS OF UPPER MANHATTAN IN NEW YORK

Body of 15-Year-Old Found in Swim Pool

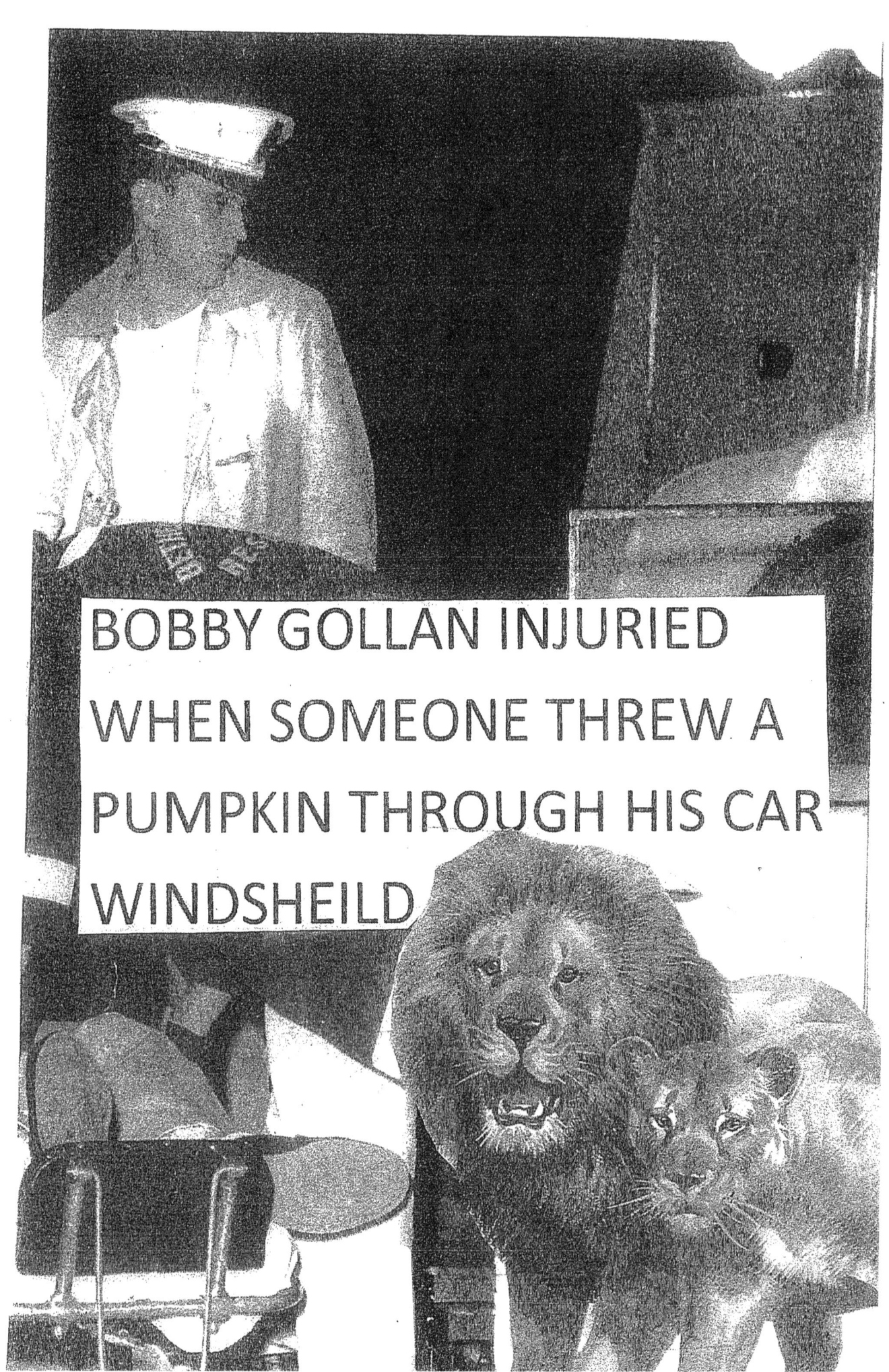

TRAIN WRECK

ALL THOUGH SOME OF IT HAD BEEN CLEARED AWAY, WE SAW ALL THE REMAINING WRECKAGE LEFT IN THE BASEMENT INCLUDING SOME OF THE TRAIN CARS AND ONE OF THE TWO LOCOMOTIVES, I DON'T REMEMBER HOW MANY OF THOSE THERE WERE NOW

THE ALL-TIME TRAIN WRECK IN WASHINGTON DC IN THE EARLY 1950s

WHERE MY FRIEND TOMMY CAMP AND I WENT TO THAT NIGHT OR MAYBE THE NEXT

A LARGE BIRD IS PERCHED ON THE SHOULDER OF A FIRE FIGHTER

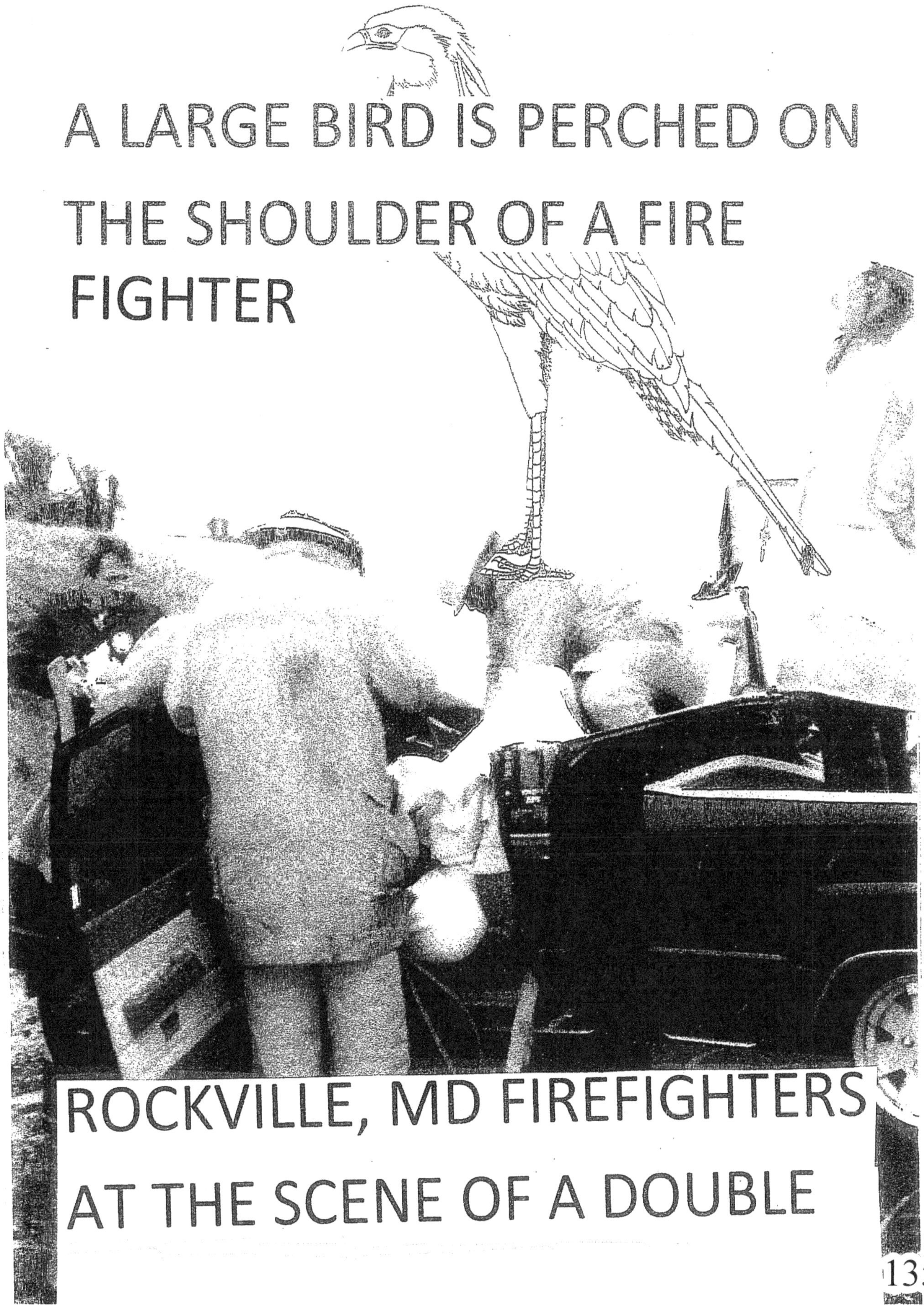

ROCKVILLE, MD FIREFIGHTERS AT THE SCENE OF A DOUBLE

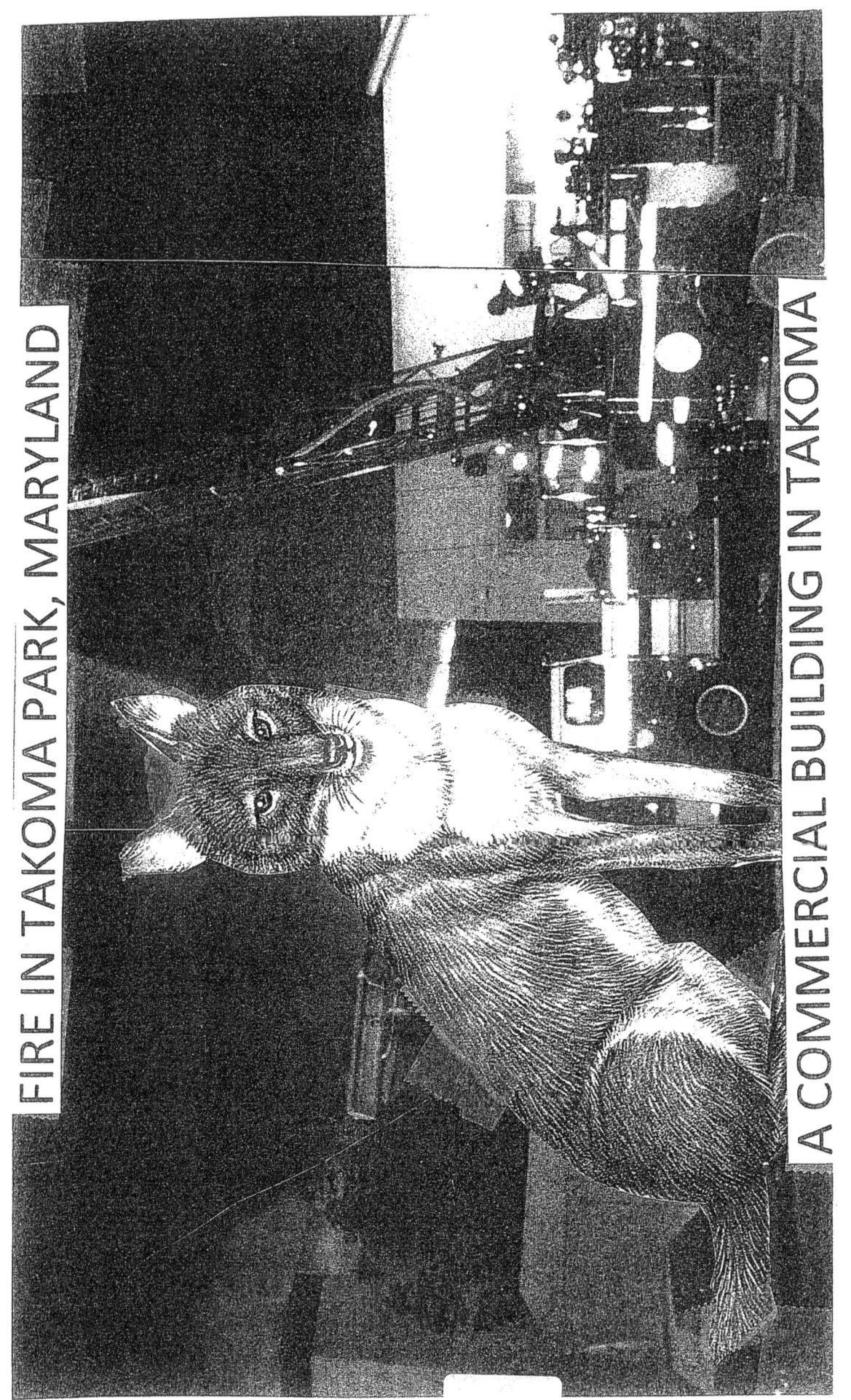

THE LIBERTY MILL FIRE IN 1972

IN 1972 I WAS RUN OVER BY A HEAVY CRANE TRUCK AND THAT IS WHY I WAS ON CRUTCHES WHEN I WENT TO THE BIG FIRE AT THE LIBERTY MILL FIRE WITH MY SON DANNY JR AND DAUGHTER DEANA.

THE OLD LIBERTY MILL IS DESTROYED IN GERMANTOWN,

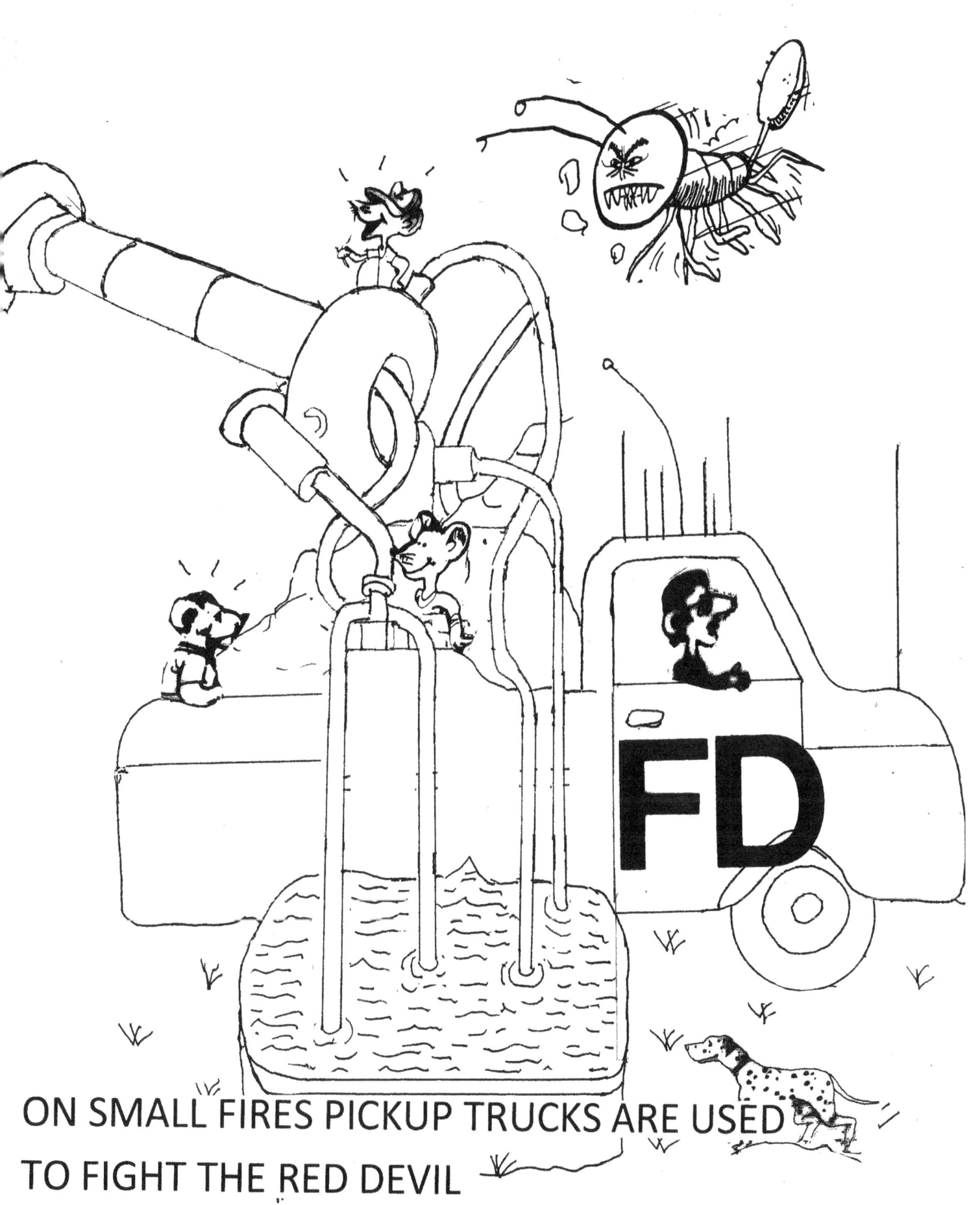

THE PIG TOWN FIRE IN BALTIMORE, MD IN THE 1980s BURNED DOWN A LARGE NUMBER OF BUILDINGS

FATAL, TREE FELL ONTO 2 PASSING CARS
WHEN A TREE FELL ONTO BOTH OF THEM
KILLING ONE OF THE DRIVERS

DANNY, TURTLE RICHARD
BOBBY, BILLY, AND BILLY
HUNTER
FITZGERALD AND OTHERS

FATAL TRUCK WRECK IN PG COUNTY

OFF-DUTY FIREFIGHTERS RELAXING BETWEEN FIGHTING FIRES

FIRE GUYS AT THE FAMOUS AND BREATH-TAKING SKULL LAKE

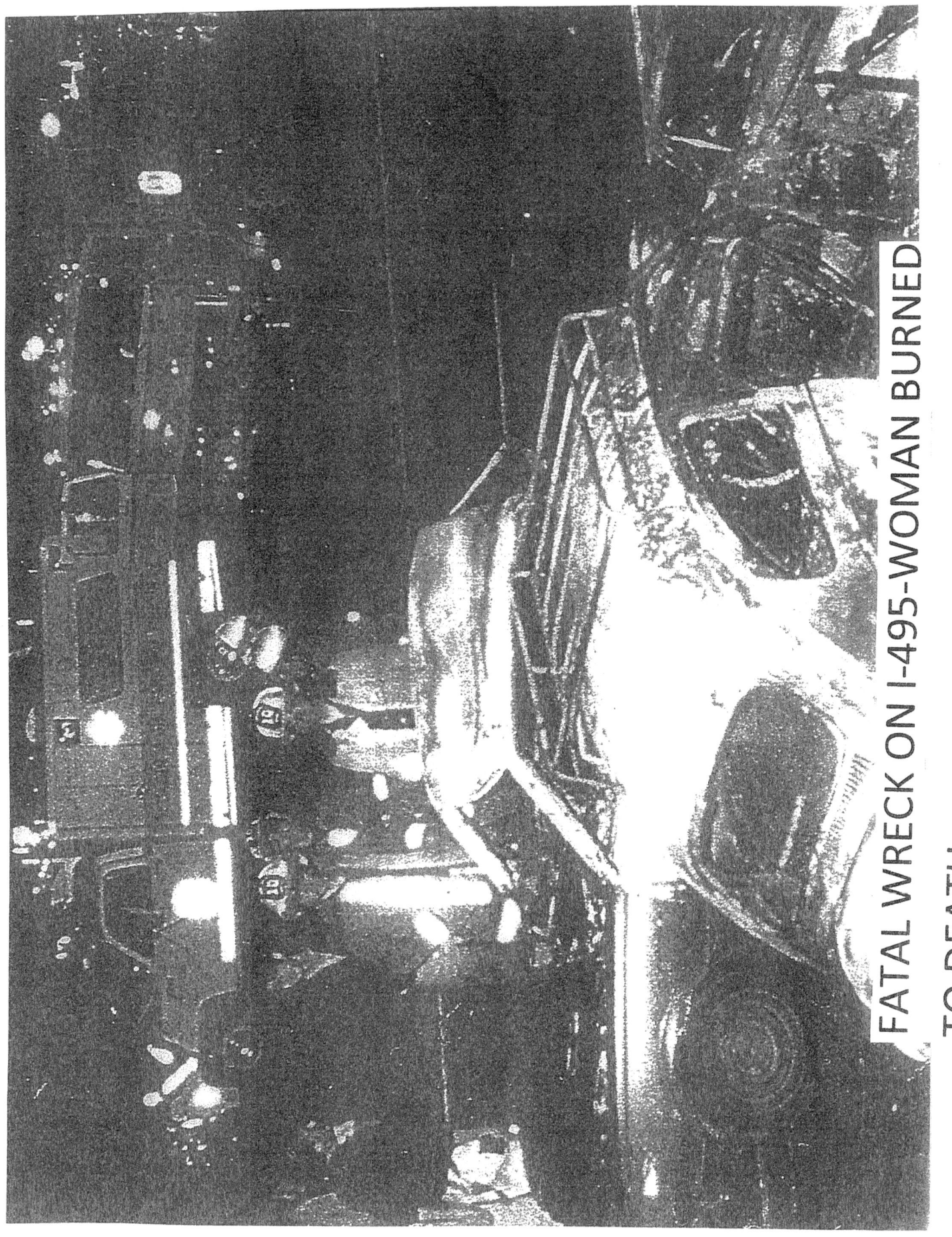

FATAL WRECK ON I-495-WOMAN BURNED TO DEATH

DANNY AND HERBY CARPENTER AND OTHERS AT LARGE BETHESDA, MD FIRE

DANNY, BOBBY, RICHARD HUNTER, BILLY FITZ, TURTLE AND A BUNCH OF SQUAD GUYS AT FATAL 495 WRECK KILLING ABOUT 5 VICTIMS

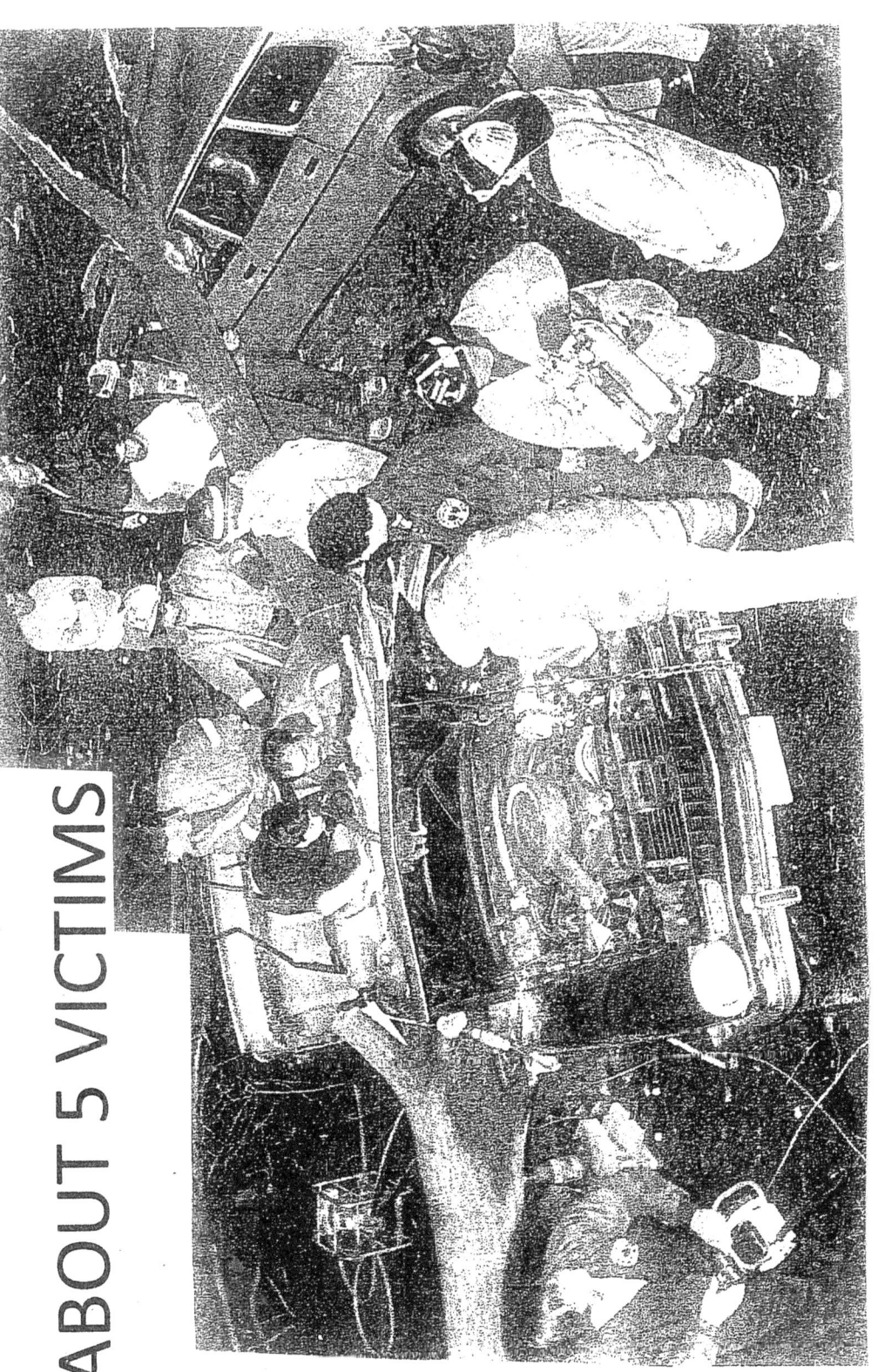

9 Area Navy Reservists Die in Crash Of Patrol Plane in Prince George's

Nine Navy reservists died yesterday when their SP2E Neptune patrol plane crashed and exploded in a small field 3½ miles southeast of Upper Marlboro in Prince George's County.

The Navy said the men all from the Washington area, had just taken off from Andrews Air Force base on a five-hour training flight. The crash site is about seven miles east of the base.

Bits of metal, clothing, and an unopened parachute littered the crash site—a 200 to 300 yard area east of the impact.

The area, a few hundred yards from Croom Station, Md., was cordoned off for an hour after the crash while Prince George's and Air Force firemen poured water and foam on the debris at the ten-foot deep crater dug by plane.

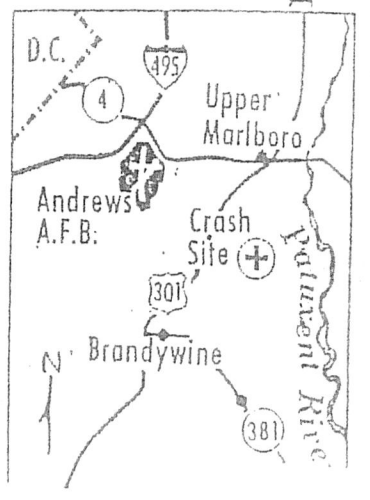

SITE OF CRASH — A cross marks the location where Navy plane crashed yesterday, killing nine persons.

The 11 Alarm fire at the Gulf Oil Refinery in South Philadelphia

A 20-ton dump truck turned over on top of my truck on route 495

DANNY AT A 2ND ALARM FIRE IN THE BRONX

A woman is killed when she drives underneath a dump truck

154

A TRUCK HIT A TRAIN IN CHEVY CHASE, MD

GERMANTOWN, MD GROCERY STORE DESTROYED IN THE 1960s

A bus on the way to the race track crashes into a bridge on route 70 near Fredrick killing 7 passengers

PIER 39 IN SAN FRANCISCO

4 Metro Workers Die in Chevy Chase Circle Crash

A LOT OF FATAL'S ON THE BELTWAY ONE NIGHT IN CHEVY CHASE

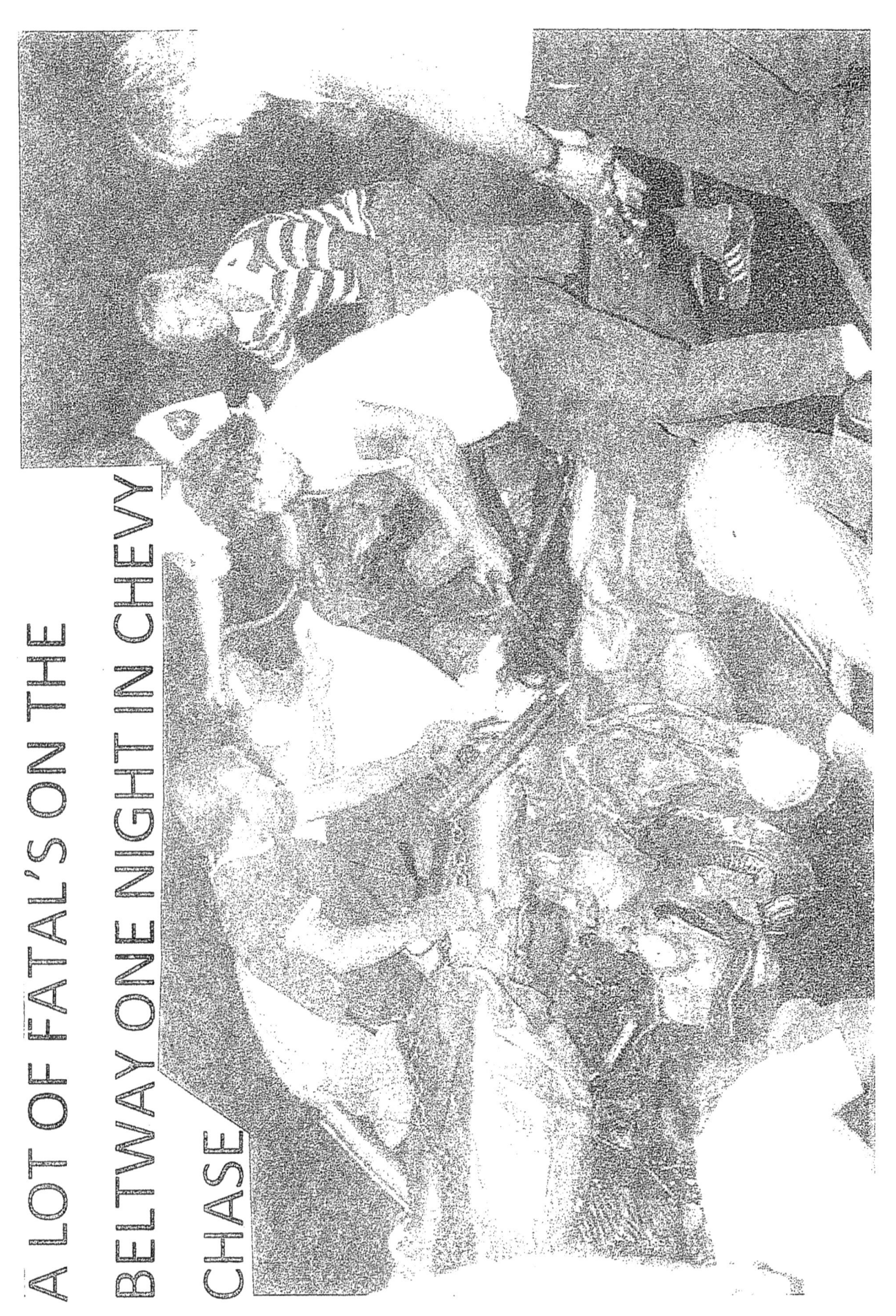

FIREFIGHTERS ENTERING THE BACK DOOR OF A FIREHOUSE

A LARGE BUILDING BURNS DOWN IN THE HEART OF GAITHERSBURG, MD

A BAT FLYING OVER THE KANN'S DEPARTMENT STORE AS IT IS BEING DESTROYED IN A MAJOR WASHINGTON FIRE

A LUMBER YARD BURNS DOWN IN ROCKY MOUNT, NC

3 VICTIMS BURNED TO DEATH IN THEIR SMALL CAR AFTER A BUS RAN INTO IT

10,000 GALLONS OF FUEL OIL EXPLODED AND IS BURNING ON INTERSTATE I-270

THE DRIVER SURVIVED

DANNY AT LADDER 124 IN BUSHWICK, BROOKLYN ACE THE MASCOT DOG IN 1980

ACE CHEWING ON A LARGE BONE

OIL HAS BEEN LOCATED BY THE MICE

A LONE WOLF APPEARING AT A WORKING FIRE IN LOWER BROOKLYN

A TRUCK TRANSPORTING FIREFIGHTERS TO SOUTHERN CALIFORNIA TO FIGHT WILDFIRES

Truck Overturned in Gaithersburg, MD

3-SNAKE INSPECTORS OUT DOING THEIR JOB ONE SUN-FILLED DAY INSPECTING SNAKES

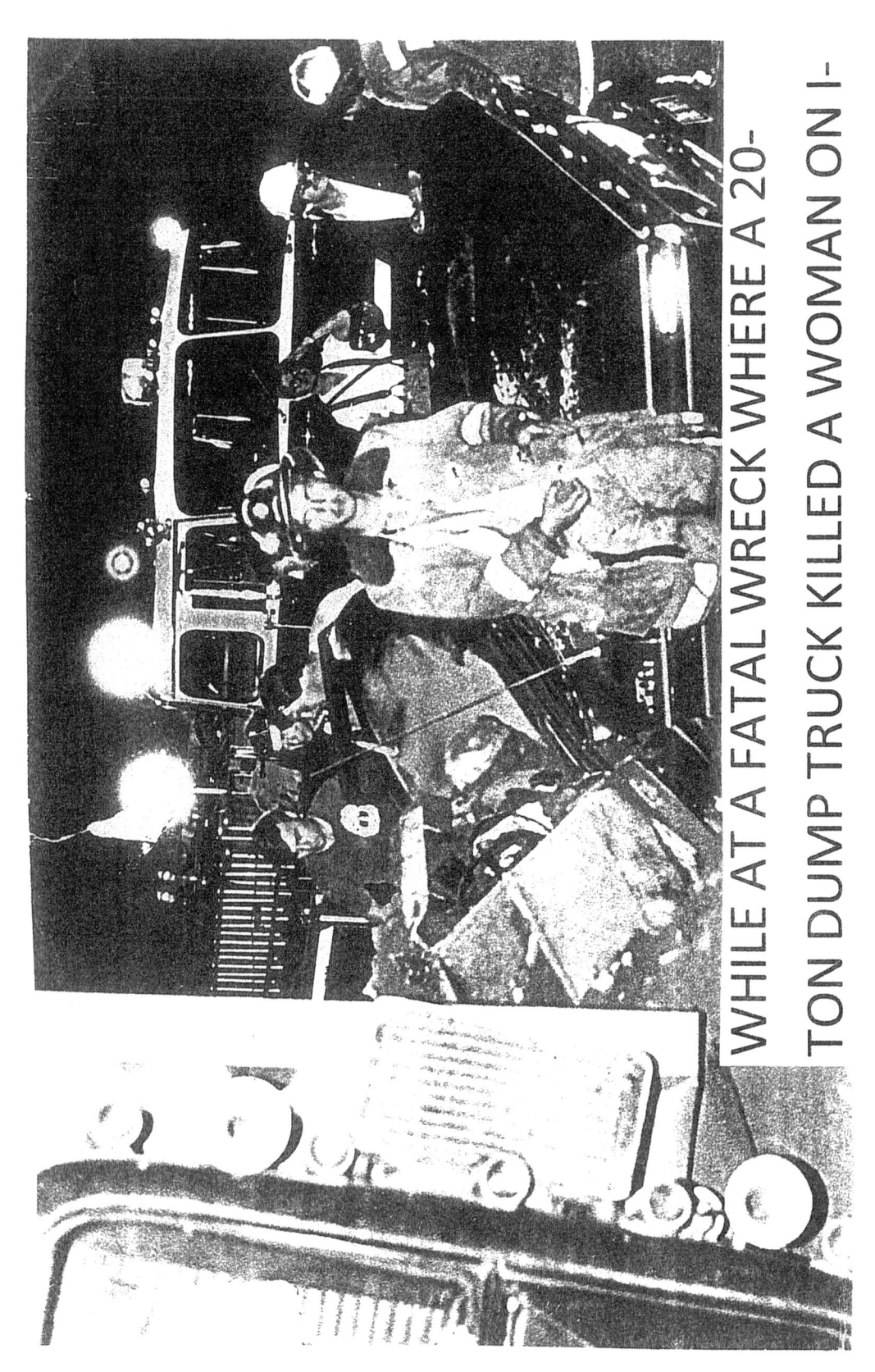

WHILE AT A FATAL WRECK WHERE A 20-TON DUMP TRUCK KILLED A WOMAN ON I-495 ANOTHER 20-TON TRUCK SPILLED OVER ONTO MY PICKUP TRUCK CRUSHING MY

FIREFIGHTER'S PERFORMING ALLIGATOR DRILLS. THAT MEANS THAT THEY JUMP

INTO THE WATER AND TEACH THE FELLOW A FEW TRICKS AND BY DOING SO WILL BUILD UP CONFIDENCE TO ADVOID BEING EATEN UP

VICTIM DROVE HIS CAR OFF A BRIDGE ONTO SOME RAILROAD TRACKS WHERE IT WAS STRUCK BY A TRAIN

OIL TANKS ON FIRE IN NEWARK, NJ–FIRE BURNED FOR 3 DAYS

THE FIRE AT THE LIBERTY MILL

A GORILLIA TOY STORE GOES UP IN FLAMES IN DETROIT, MD

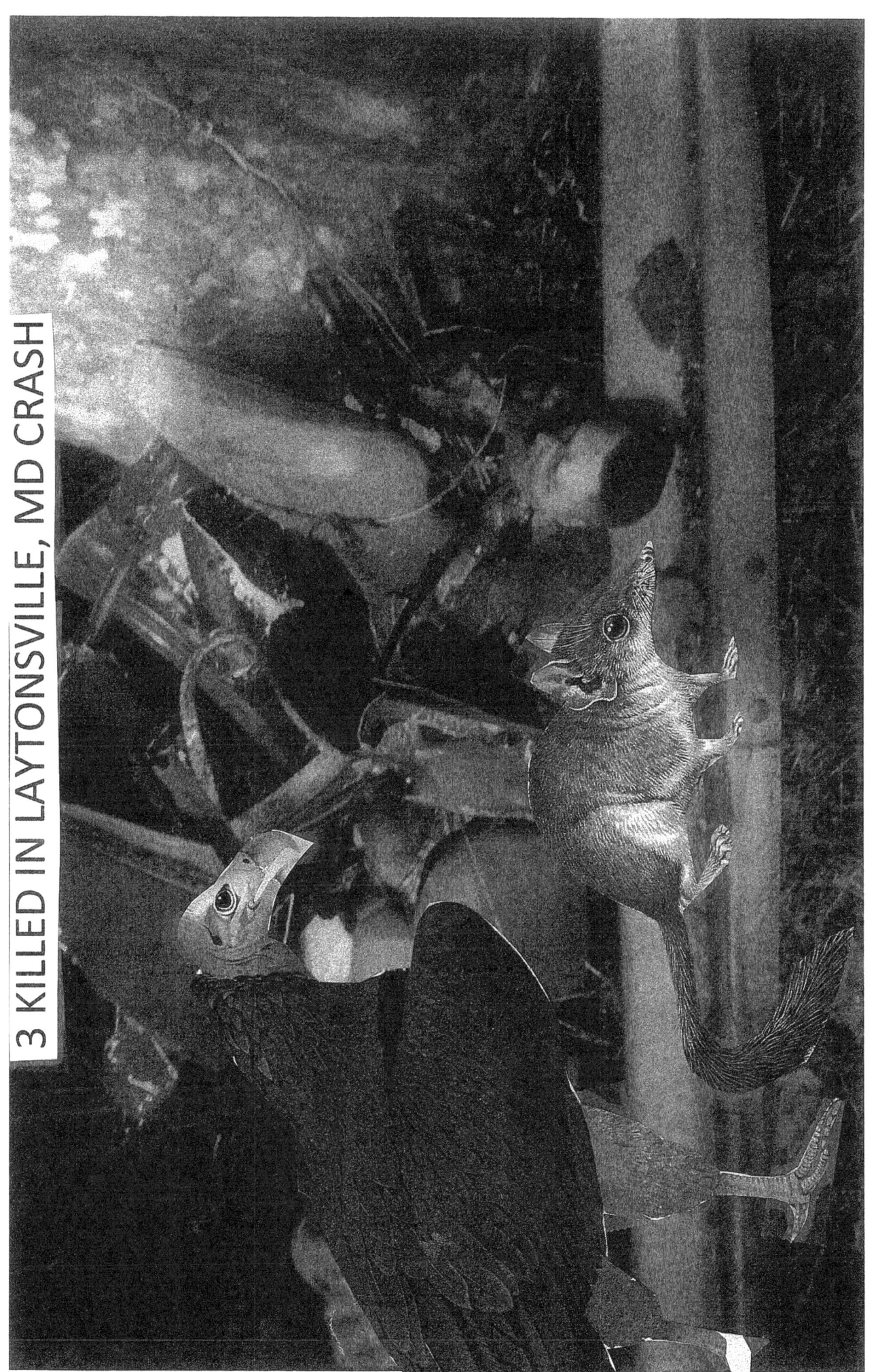

A LARGE FIRE IN WALKERSVILLE, MD WHEN A FEED MILL BURNS DOWN

AS THE CITY-BLOCK KANN'S STORE IS CONSUMED BY FLAMES IN WASHINGTON A LONE BIRD SITS ON A FIRENGINE TO TAKE IT ALL IN

A GOOD-LOOKING KANGAROO COMES OUT TO WATCH ONE OF THREE LARGE TANKS OF OIL BURN

Suicide in Laytonsville, MD – Car Ran into Barn, Which Burned to the

189

Burned Body in Car

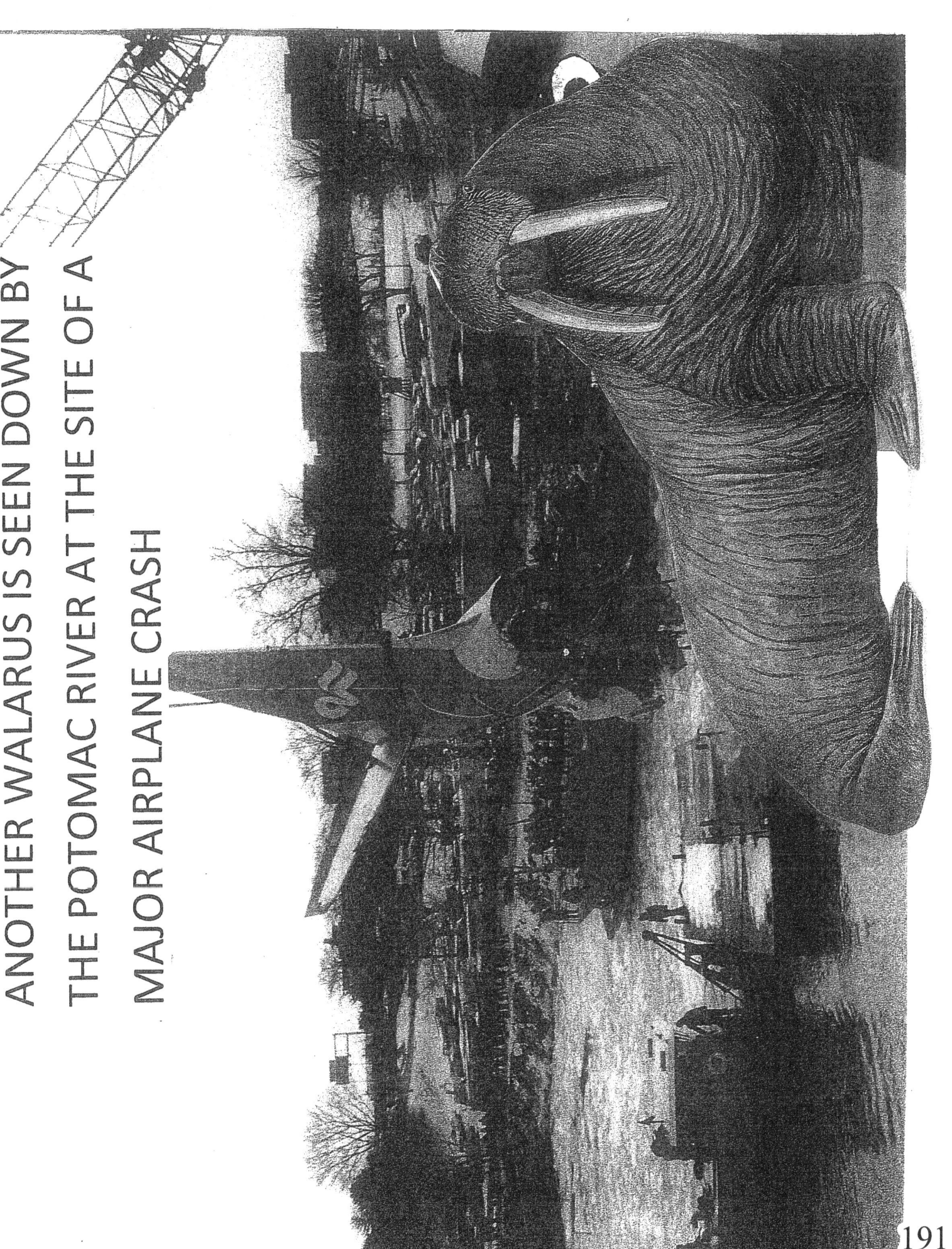

ANOTHER WALARUS IS SEEN DOWN BY THE POTOMAC RIVER AT THE SITE OF A MAJOR AIRPLANE CRASH

KANN'S DEPARTMENT STORE FIRE IN WASHINGTON, DC

BILLY FITZGERALD AND OTHERS AT A HANGING WHERE THE VICTIM HAS BEEN CUT DOWN

HUNGRY FIREFIGHTERS EATING BATBURGERS IN BETWEEN FIGHTING FIRES AND RUNNING WRECKS

DANNY, JIM BOB, AND JOE HARABSTEIN AT TRIPLE FATAL TRUCK OVERTURNED AT A BUS STOP IN KENSINGTON MD

A TERRIBLE FIRE ROARED THROUGH THE CACTUS CAFÉ ONE DAY IN MOUSETOWN

GUYS AT A PIER FIRE

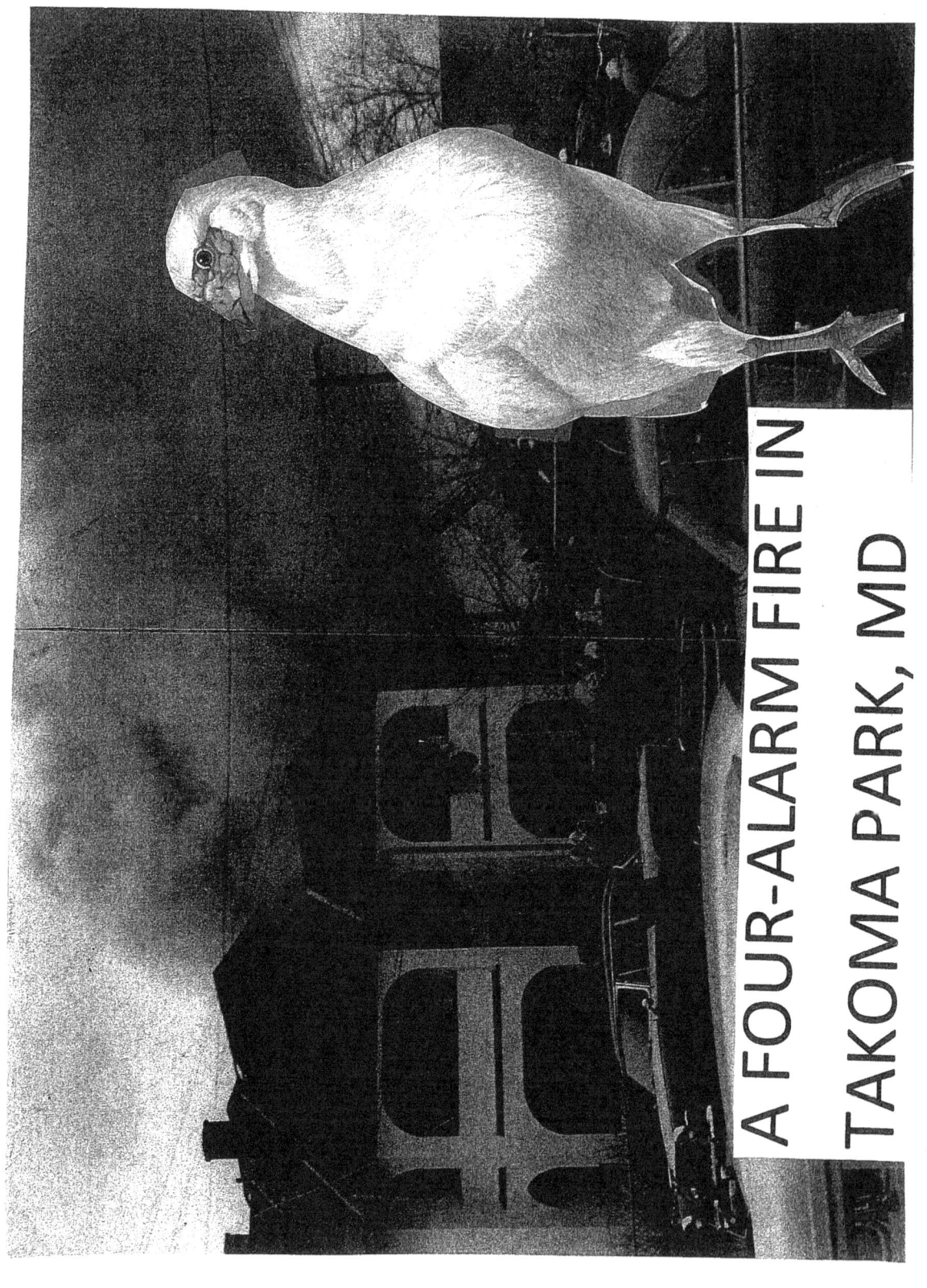

A FOUR-ALARM FIRE IN TAKOMA PARK, MD

LARGE TIGER WAS SEEN WALKING AROUND ON THE FIREGROUND

A LARGE BIRD TAKING IN THE FIRE SCENE

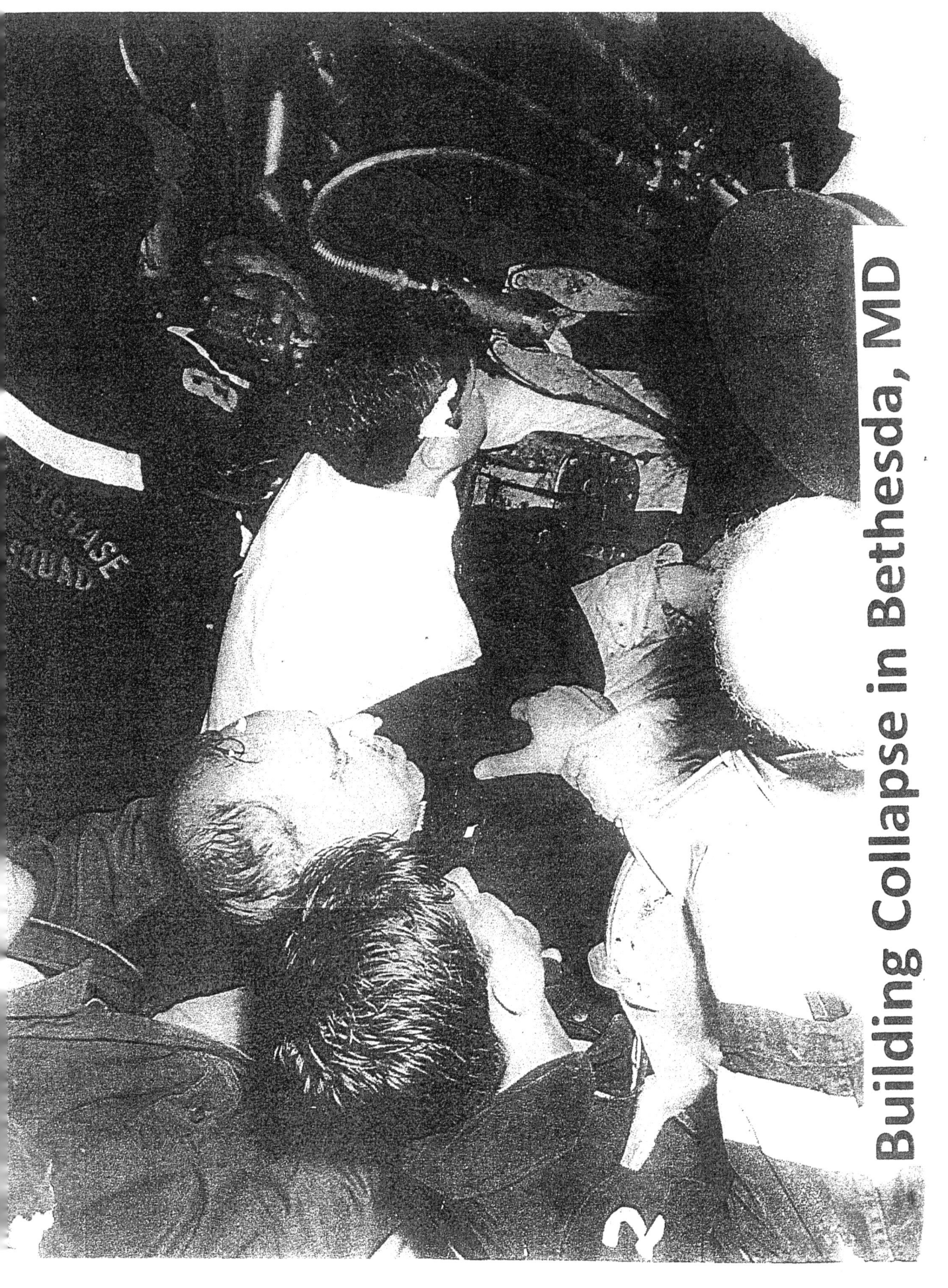

Building Collapse in Bethesda, MD

BETHESDA OIL FIRE IN 1958

ONE OF THE MOST-VISITED TOURIST ATTRACTIONS IN THE WORLD AND UP TO 17 PERSONS HAD REPORTED TO HAVE DIED WHILE PEERING AT THE MAGNIFICANT WORK OF ART BY BAXTER J CADBURY

THE PICTURE ON THE WALL-THIS AMAZING PICTURE OF WILL PINION SEEN BY MILLIONS

WOMAN KILLED IN BOYD'S MD

MILK TANKER STRUCK A TREE AND A CAR

11 FATALITIES WHEN A PASSENGER TRAIN COLLIDED WITH A TRAIN IN IN SILVER SPRING, MD

THE MARC TRAIN WAS DESTROYED AND ALL THE DEAD WERE FOUND IN ONE BURNED-OUT PASSENGER CAR

GUY HIT BY A TRAIN IN KENSINGTON, MD

THE DUDE WAS SITTING THERE DRINKING WINE ON THE TRACKS WHEN HE WAS STRUCK

THE GERMANTOWN STORE BURNS DOWN A LONG TIME AGO, AND IS NEVER REBUILT

SOME OF THE GUYS
FIREFIGHTERS

WHEN THEY ARE NOT FIGHTING FIRES AND SAVING LIVES THEY ARE WORKING AND ROUGHHOUSING AND KEEPING IN SHAPE

FIRE DEPARTMENTS HAVE THE TRAINING CENTERS TO PRACTICE LIVE EARTHQUAKE DRILLS TO GAIN FURTHUR KNOWLEDGE ABOUT FALLING STRUCTURES

WHEN YOU GO OUT THE FIREHOUSE RESPONDING ON AN EMERGENCY RUN, YOU JUST NEVER KNOW IF YOU WILL EVER RETURN AND SEE YOUR FAMILY AGAIN

FIREFIGHTERS USED TO SEND KIDS TO CAMP SNOUT IN THE SUMMER, NO LONGER, THINGS GOT OUT OF HAND OR PAW, BAD THINGS STARTED TO OCCUR

Drowning Victim in Potomac River

NOT ALL SEA TURTLES ARE THAT FRIENDLY. HERE IN THE POTOMAC RIVER, NEAR CABIN JOHN WHERE REMAINS OF AN ELDERLY SKELETON OUT BIRD-WATCHING ARE FOUND

VICTIM STILL UNDER 20-TON SLAB OF CONCRETE AT NIH IN BETHESDA, MD

Large Fire in Bronx, NY

Fatal Truck Wreck on I-95 in Beltsville, MD

A FATAL WRECK IN BETHESDA, MD

BOBBY AND DANNY AT A FREIGHT TRAIN WRECK WHERE A NUMBER OF COWS WERE KILLED IN ROCKVILLE, MD

ONE OF SEVERAL FIREBOATS AT A LARGE FIRE IN THE BRONX, NY

MULTI-ALARM FIRE IN TAKOMA PARK, MD

DANNY AND A CLOSE FRIEND ON A RIVERBOAT ON THE MISSISSIPPI RIVER BY THE ARCH

A DROWNING IN THE POTOMAC RIVER, CABIN JOHN, MD

RACE TRACK FIRE IN UPPER MARLBORO, MD

FATAL WRECK 3 KILLED ON THE INTERSTATE, FIREFIGHTER USING ICE TONGS TO REMOVE DECEASED WOMAN FROM CAR

SARA RALL AND DANNY AT FATAL WRECK ON THE INTERSTATE AND I-270

DROWNING IN THE POTOMAC RIVER

THERE WERE 3 DECEASED PERSONS IN THIS WRECK ON THE SUITLAND PARKWAY IN DC ONE NIGHT WHICH STEVE AND I WENT TO

THIS WOMAN JUMPED TO HER DEATH FROM THE 6TH FLOOR OF AN APARTMENT BUILDING ALSO KNOWN AS AN AREA CALLED THE JUMPING BELT BECAUSE OF THE LARGE NUMBER OF SUICIDES THERE THAT DO THAT TYPE OF WORK

FATAL WRECK ON I-270

A TRUCK FELL OVER ON TOP OF A CAR CRUSHING THE DRIVER TO DEATH IN CHEVY CHASE, MD

THE LIBERTY MILL IN GERMANTOWN, MD BURNS DOWN IN 1972

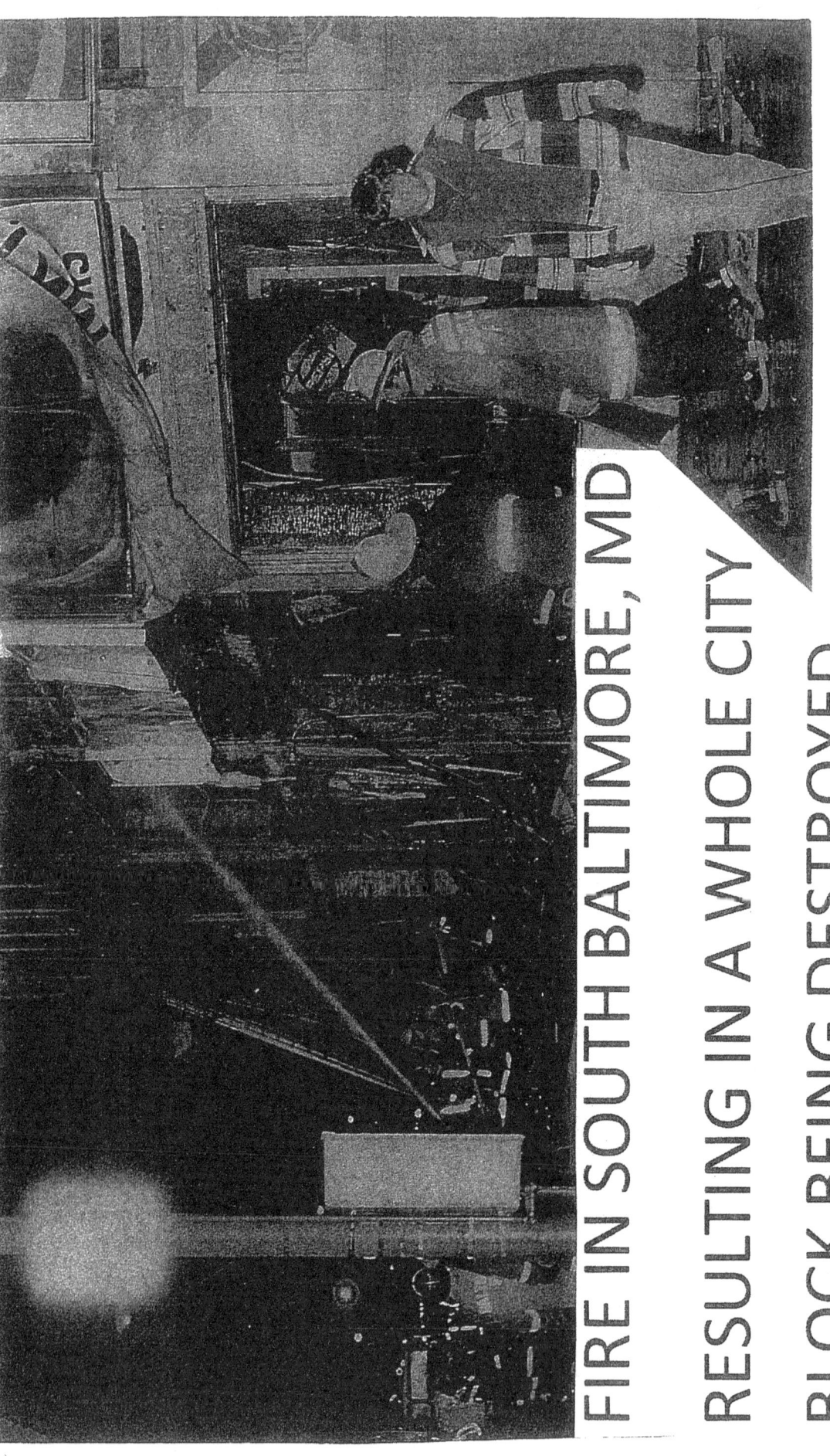

FIRE IN SOUTH BALTIMORE, MD RESULTING IN A WHOLE CITY BLOCK BEING DESTROYED

A NUMBER OF MICE TOURISTS ADMIRE THE ICE CYCLES ON ST. JOSEPH PIER LIGHTHOUSE, ON LAKE MICHIGAN ACROSS FROM CHICAGO

USED FOR LARGE FIRES IN NEW YORK CITY EACH BROUGH HAS ONE, REPLACING THE SUPER PUMPER A LONG TIME AGO

THE DRIVER OF THIS JEEP BY THE CABIN JOHN BRIDGE NEAR CABIN JOHN, MD IS KILLED

THE WASHINGTONIAN MOTEL IN GAITHERSBURG, MD IS DESTROYED IN A 4-ALARM FIRE IN THE 1970s

A TRUCK RUNS INTO A BUILDING KILLING THE DRIVER IN UPPER MARLBORO, MD

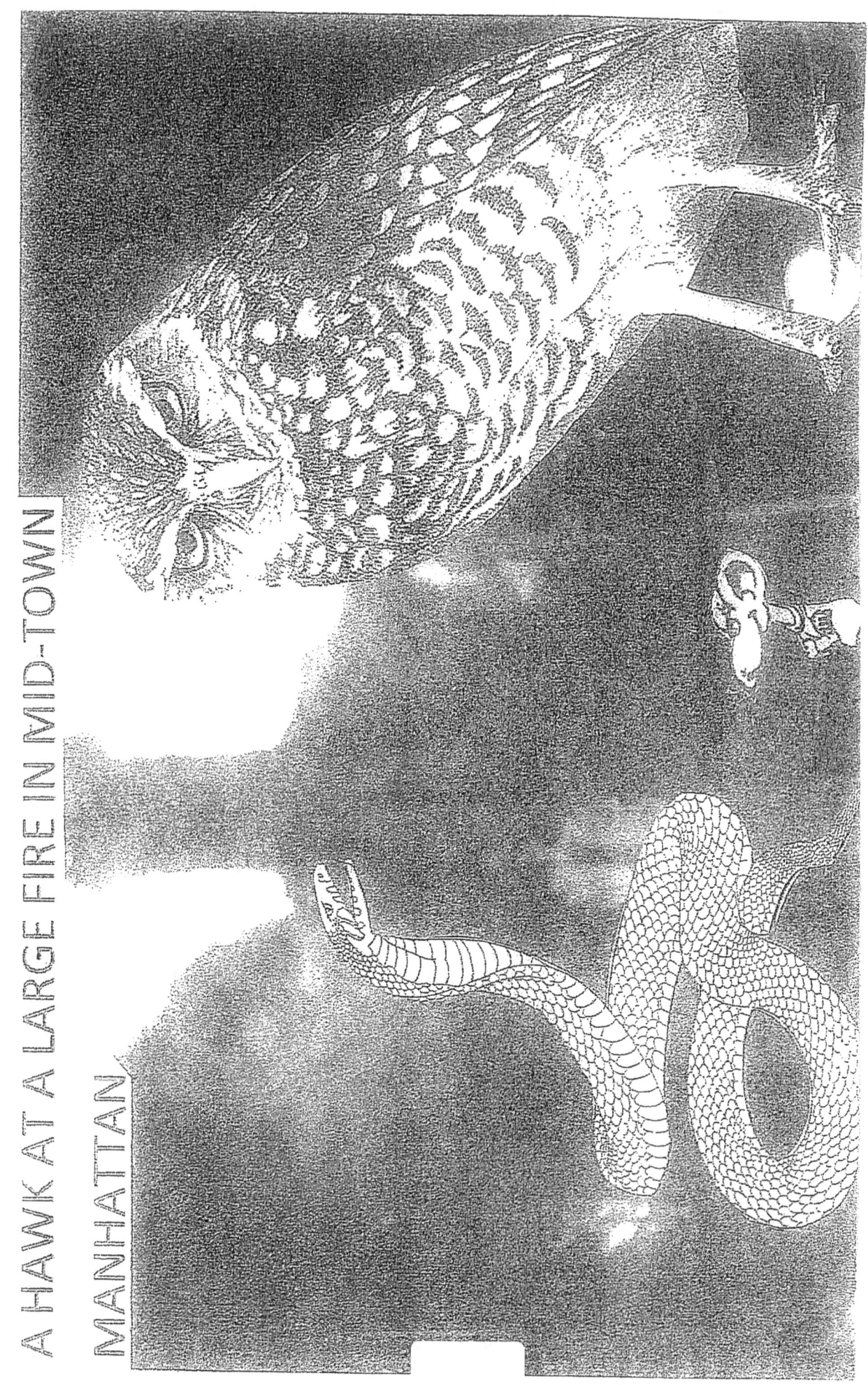

A HAWK AT A LARGE FIRE IN MID-TOWN MANHATTAN

A DRAGON AT A 5-ALARM FIRE IN THE BRONX WALKING IN THE PARKING LOT

A TREE CLIMBER WAS STRUCK IN THE HEAD BY A LARGE SECTION OF THE TREE THAT HE WAS IN THAT HE HAD JUST CUT, EVERYTHING INSIDE HIS HEAD WAS NOW ON THE GROUND AT THE BOTTOM OF THE TREE LEAVING A TOTALY EMPTY SKULL

SEVERAL GOOD-LOOKING ANIMALS ROAMING AROUND A BURNING BUILDING IN BROOKLYN

A LARGE FIRE BURNING OUT OF CONTROL NEAR HUNT'S POINT IN THE BRONX IN THE 1970s

THE WASHINGTONIAN MOTEL IN GAITHERSBURG, MD IS DESTROYED IN A 4-ALARM FIRE IN THE 1970s

DANNY AT A GREATER ALARM FIRE IN THE BRONX IN THE 1980s

SOME OF THE GUYS AT A BIKER BAR IN WASHINGTON COUNTY PARTYING

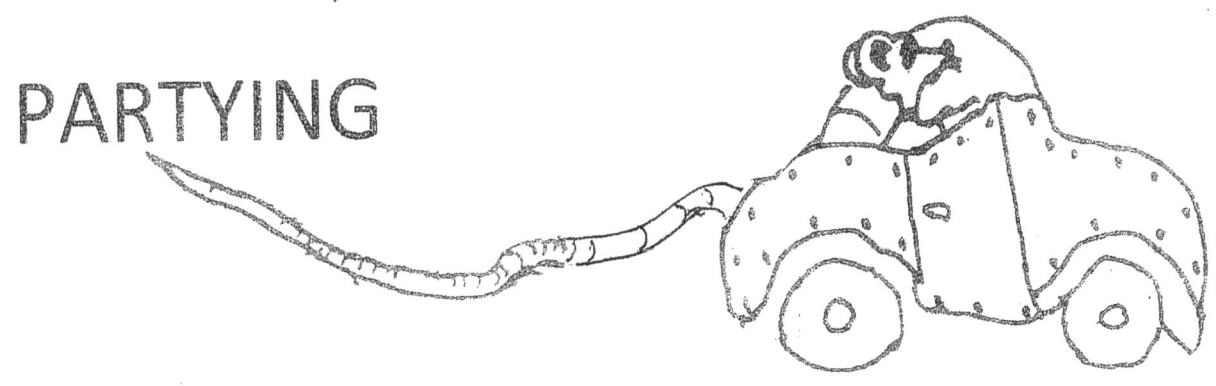

A 5-ALARM FIRE IN THE BRONX, NEW YORK

SONNY FARRINGTON AND OTHERS AT A BARN FIRE IN ROCKVILLE, MD

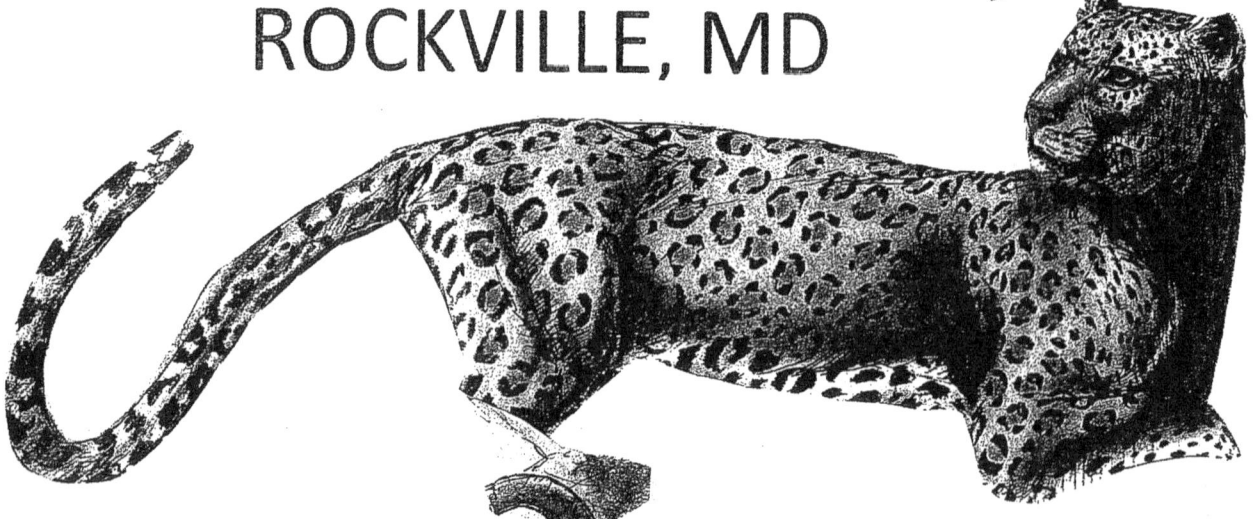

PLANE CRASH IN UPPER MARLBORO, MD
9 NAVAL RESERVIST ARE KILLED WHEN PLANE CRASHED INTO A FIELD

TWO DUDES WHO DO NOT KNOW HOW TO SWIM GO SWIMMING AND DROWN IN THE POTOMAC RIVER IN THE 1980s

Double Drowning at Great Falls Park, MD

AT THE GENERAL ALARM FIRE IN 1958 A LARGE TIGER WAS SEEN WALKING AROUND ON THE FIREGROUND

BETHESDA OIL FIRE

Oil Blaze Damage Is in Millions

GENERAL-ALARM FIRE IN MONTGOMERY COUNTY, MD

THIS FELLOW CAUSED THIS TRACTOR TRAILER, TO OVERTURN THAN IT WENT ABOUT ITS JOB EATING GRASS ALONG I-95 IN NORTH CAROLINA

A WALARUS AT A BUILDING FIRE IN NEW YORK CITY

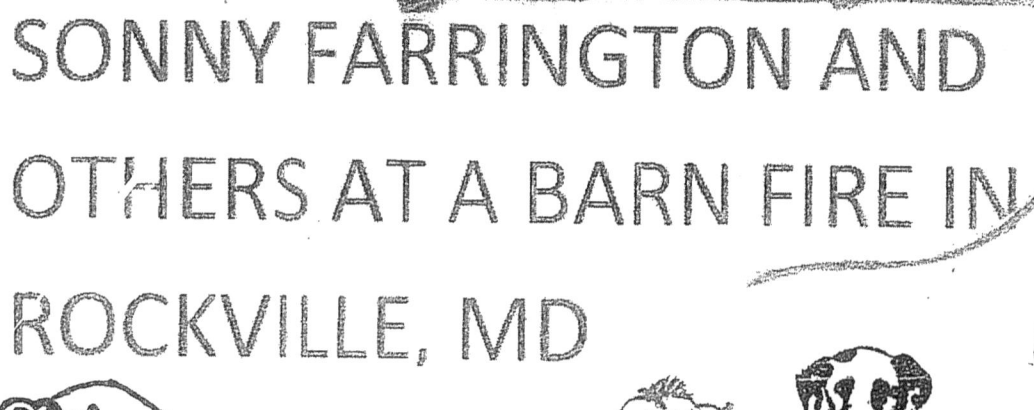

SONNY FARRINGTON AND OTHERS AT A BARN FIRE IN ROCKVILLE, MD

TWO KIDS WALKING DOWN THE RAILROAD TRACKS IN KENSINGTON, MD LISTNING TO TRANSISTOR RADIO WERE RUN OVER BY A FREIGHT TRAIN

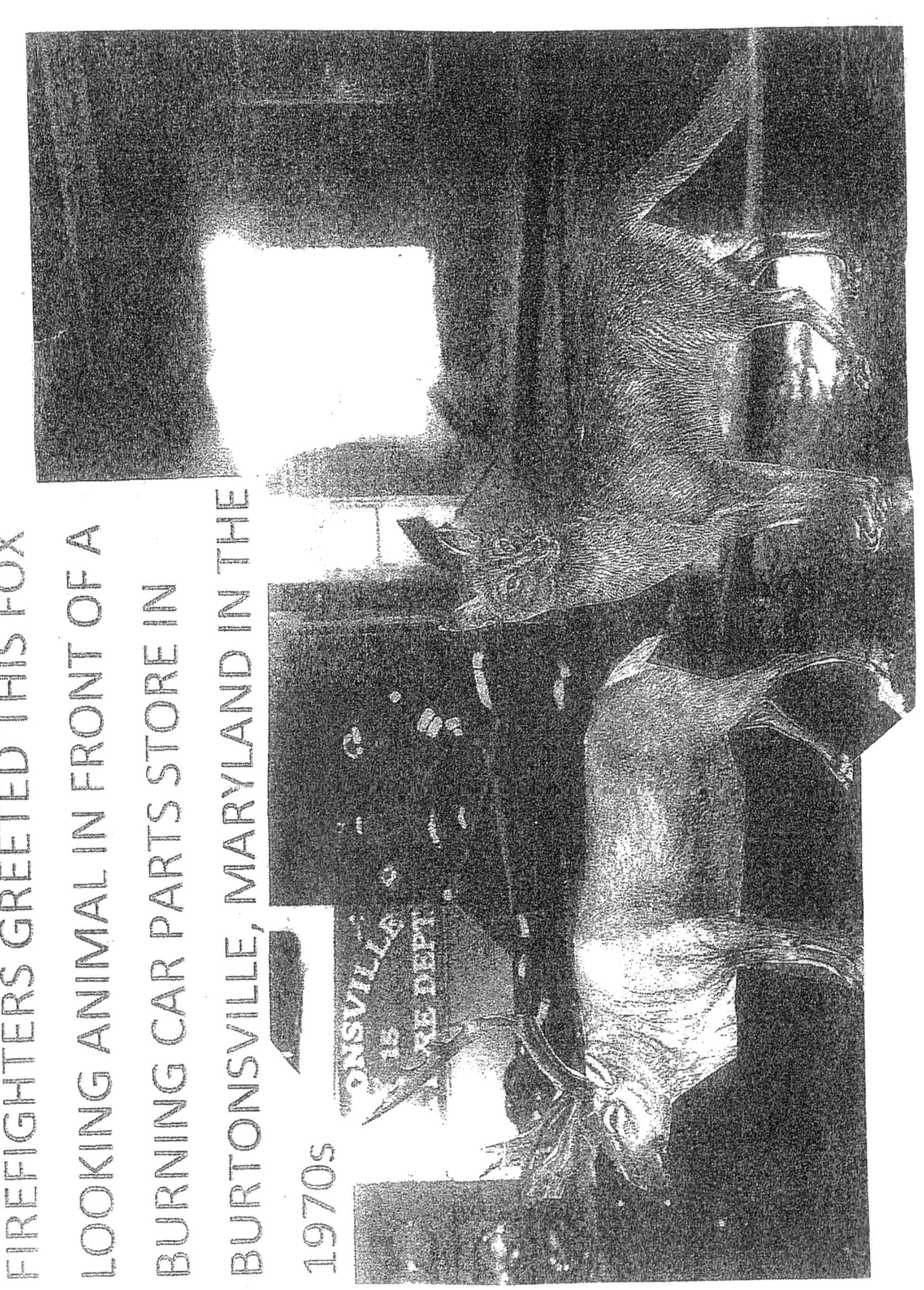

FIREFIGHTERS GREETED THIS FOX LOOKING ANIMAL IN FRONT OF A BURNING CAR PARTS STORE IN BURTONSVILLE, MARYLAND IN THE 1970S

An elephant on the fireground at a large fire in Gaithersburg, Maryland being directed by the fire chief

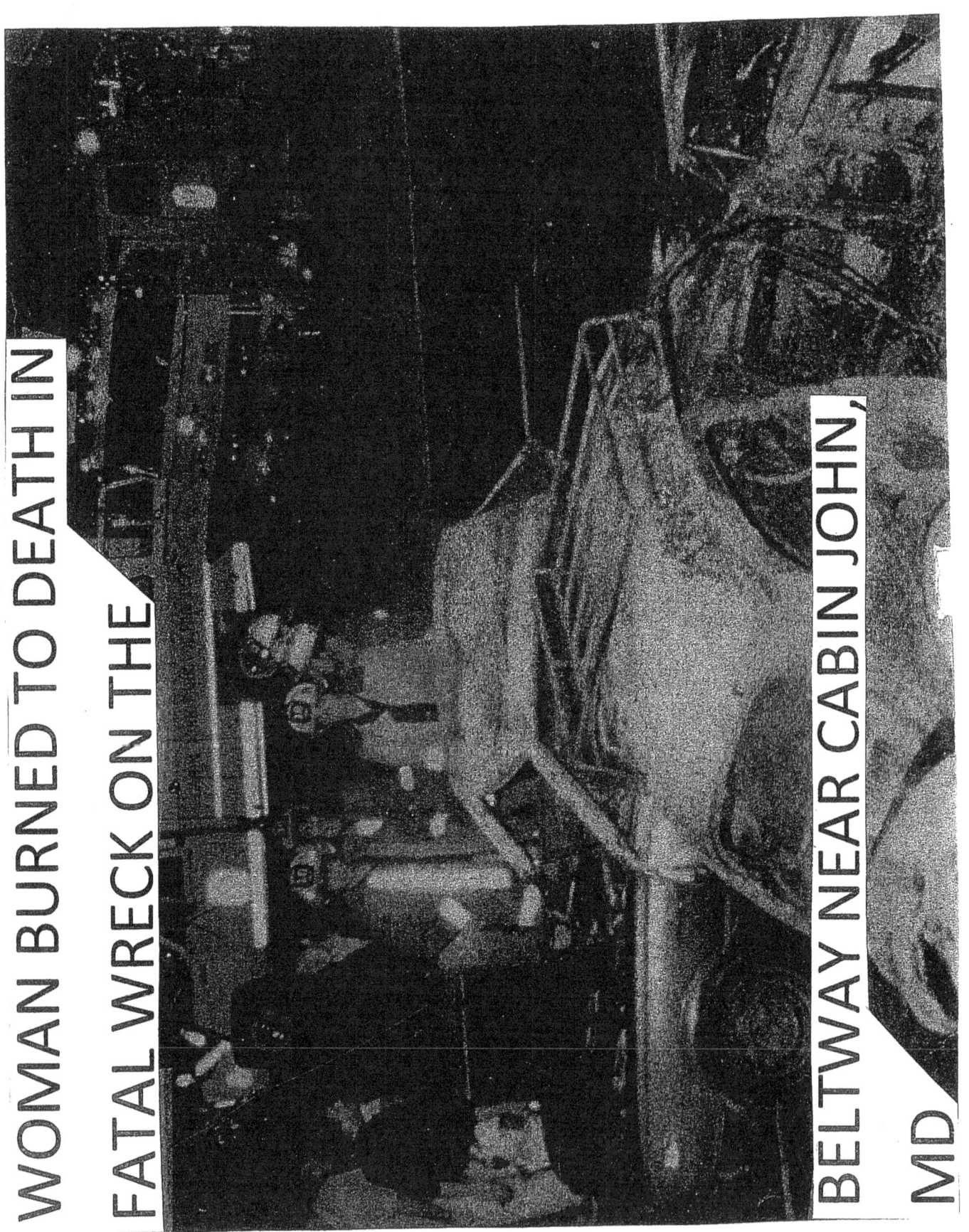

WOMAN BURNED TO DEATH IN FATAL WRECK ON THE BELTWAY NEAR CABIN JOHN, MD

2 KILLED IN GATHERSBURG, MD WRECK

A BEAR IS SEEN LOOKING AT A FATAL WRECK AFTER AN OIL TANKER THAT DID NOT EXPLODE FELL OFF THE CABIN JOHN BRIDGE NEAR CABIN JOHN BRIDGE   A GOOD-LOOKING BEAR

A TIGER HAS THE RUN OF A HOUSING PROJECT WHILE NEW YORK FIREFIGHTERS BATTLE A BUILDING ON FIRE

PENTAGON FIRE
1959

THE PENTAGON FIRE IN 1959 WENT TO 5-ALARMS AND 40 FIREFIGHTERS HAD TO RETIRE FOR MEDICAL REASONS

A HOUSE FIRE IN CHEVY CHASE, MD THAT BURNED THE ROOF OFF

NY Factory Fire in the Bronx, NY

Train Crashed into Union Station in D.C. In the early 50s and no fatalities

277

A NEW CONCEPT IN RESCUE WORK FISH COPTERS ARE ABOUT TO TAKE THE PLACE OF THE HELICOPTER IN MANY CITIES IN AMERICA

Body Discovered on Rocks, North of Key Bridge, DC

Unidentified Man's Body Recovered

STUDENT FIREFIGHTERS LEARNING ABOUT THE MOON, SOME STARS AND THE PLANET SATURN, IN CASE THE NEED EVER COMES TO HAVE TO GO THERE AND FIGHT FIRES, POSSIBLE IN THE FUTURE

General Alarm Oil Fire in Bethesda, MD

General Alarm Oil Fire in Glen Echo, MD

A FIRE CHIEF AT THE SCENE OF THE LARGEST FIRE IN MONTGOMERY COUNTY HISTORY

THE 1958 OIL FIRE- THE FIRE CHIEF WAITING FOR FIRE ENGINES TO ARRIVE

DROWNING VICTIM
VICTIM ATTACHED SEVERAL CINDER BLOCKS TO HIS BODY AND JUMPED INTO A SWIMMING POOL ONE NIGHT, UNABLE TO RISE, HE DROWNED AND WAS FOUND THE NEXT DAY LAYING ON THE BOTTOM

THE DOG SURVIVED FORTUNATELY

VICTIM THREW HIS DOG IN THE WATER AND SHOT HIMSELF,

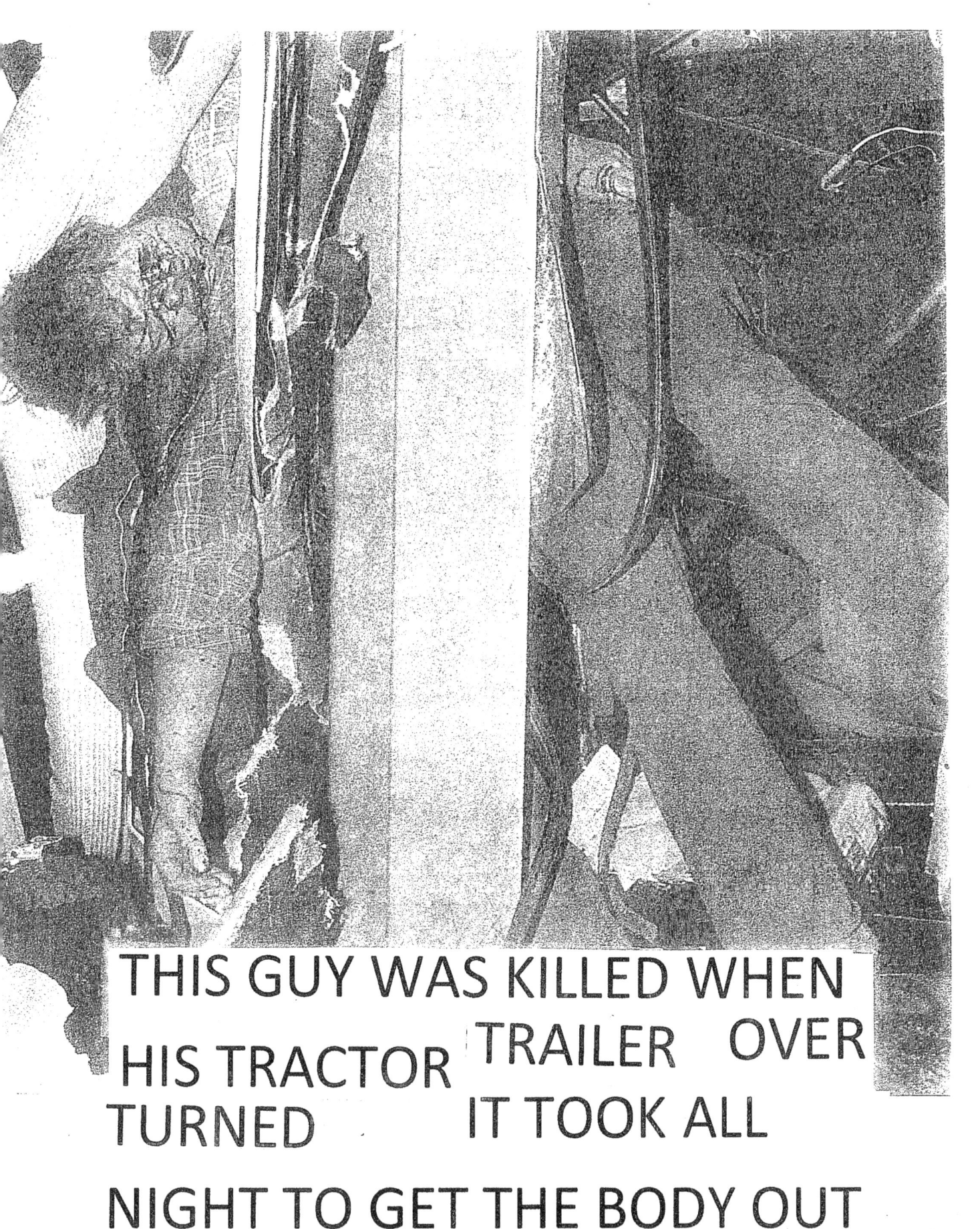

THE LIBERTY MILL IN GERMANTOWN, MD BURNED DOWN IN 1972

2 ELDERLY WOMAN RUN INTO THE BACK OF A DUMP TRUCK IN BETHESDA, MD AND ARE KILLED

2 WOMAN KILLED IN CABIN JOHN WRECK

2 Die in Md. Home Explosion

2 TEENS BURNED UP WHEN THEIR CAR HIT THE SIDE OF A BRIDGE IN VIRGINIA

(3 FATALS ON I-95)

DANNY AT THE 2-ALARM HIGHS STORE FIRE IN CHEVY CHASE, MD

GASOLINE TANKER FELL OFF THE CABIN JOHN BRIDGE KILLING THE DRIVER

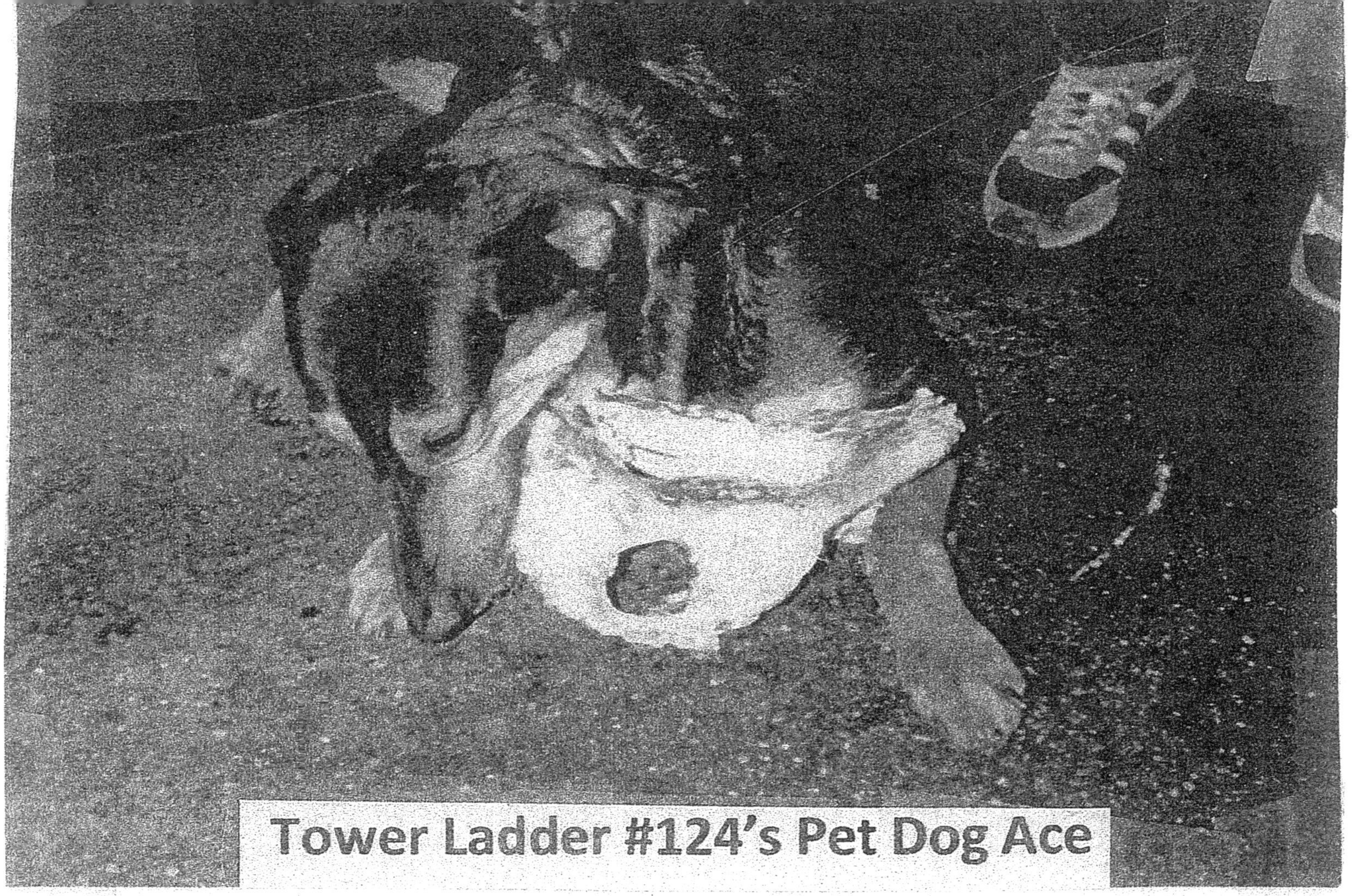

Tower Ladder #124's Pet Dog Ace

Maryland

PICTURE OF THE PLANE

21 DIE IN $50-MILLION AIR FORCE CRASH IN WALKERSVILLE, MD

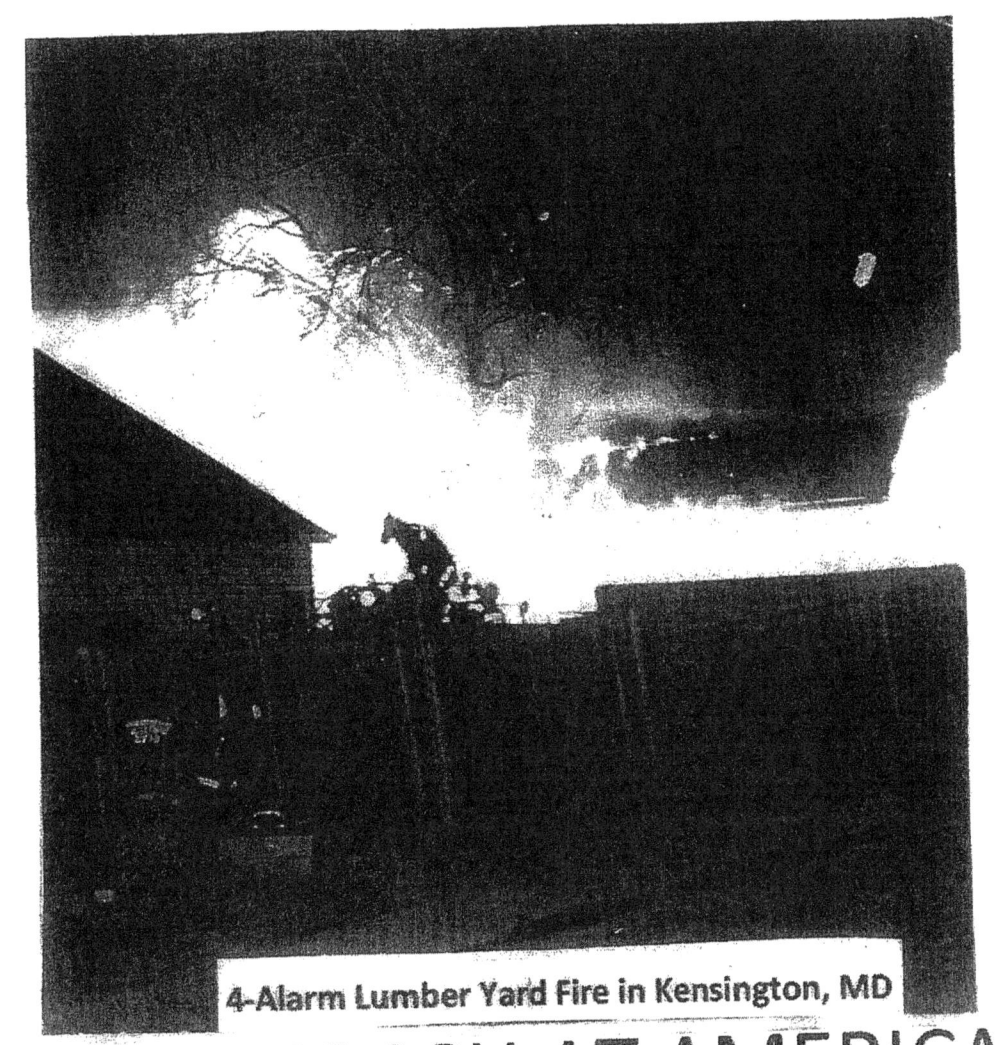

4-Alarm Lumber Yard Fire in Kensington, MD

A PLANE CRASH AT AMERICAN UNIVERSITY, ABOUT 5 PERSONS ARE KILLED

A FEED MILL BURNS DOWN IN 1972

SOME TYPE OF SEA MONSTER SIGHTED IN THE POTOMAC RIVER AT HIGH NOON ONE DAY

Freight Train Wreck in Pohick, VA

3 KIDS KILLED THE LAST DAY OF SCHOOL IN AN AUTO ACCIDENT

A 6-STORY BUILDING IN OWENS MILLS, MD BURNS DOWN

SAGUARO NATIONAL PARK BOTH EAST AND WEST IN AZ

MONUMENT VALLEY, AZ

FATAL WRECK ON KEY BRIDGE AS CAR PLUNGES INTO THE POTOMAC RIVER

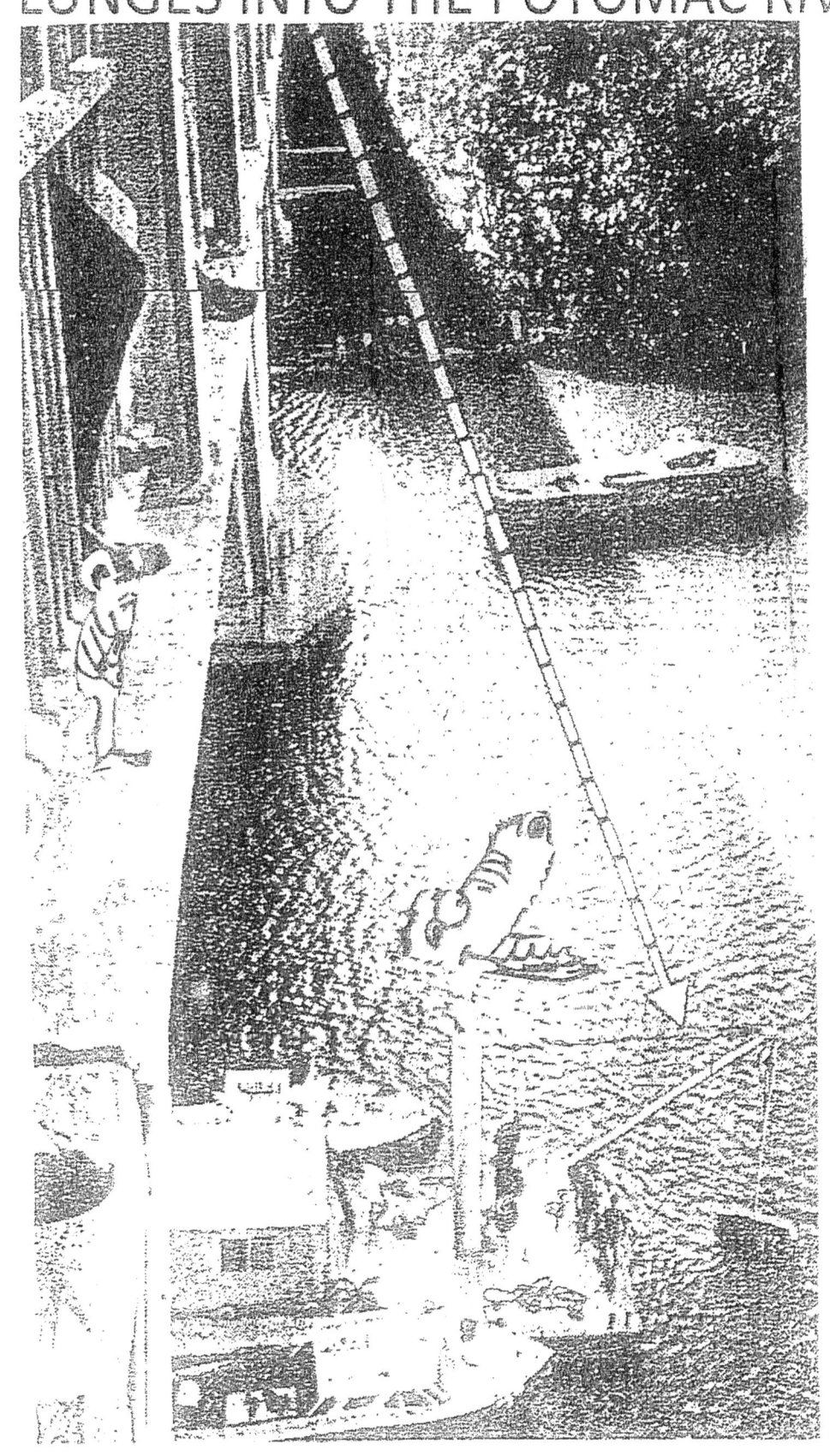

A LUMBER YARD BURNS DOWN IN ROCKY MOUNT, NC

DANNY AND HERBY CARPENTER AND OTHERS AT LARGE BETHESDA, MD FIRE

FATAL TRUCK WRECK ON THE CABIN JOHN BRIDGE

THIS GUY WAS FOUND DROWNED ON TOP OF A DAM IN SILVER SPRING, MD

TOM PARSONS, MYSELF AND ANOTHER SQUAD GUY AND A LION AT A CAVE-IN IN DC

EXTRACTING ANOTHER (FLOATER) FROM THE POTOMAC RIVER

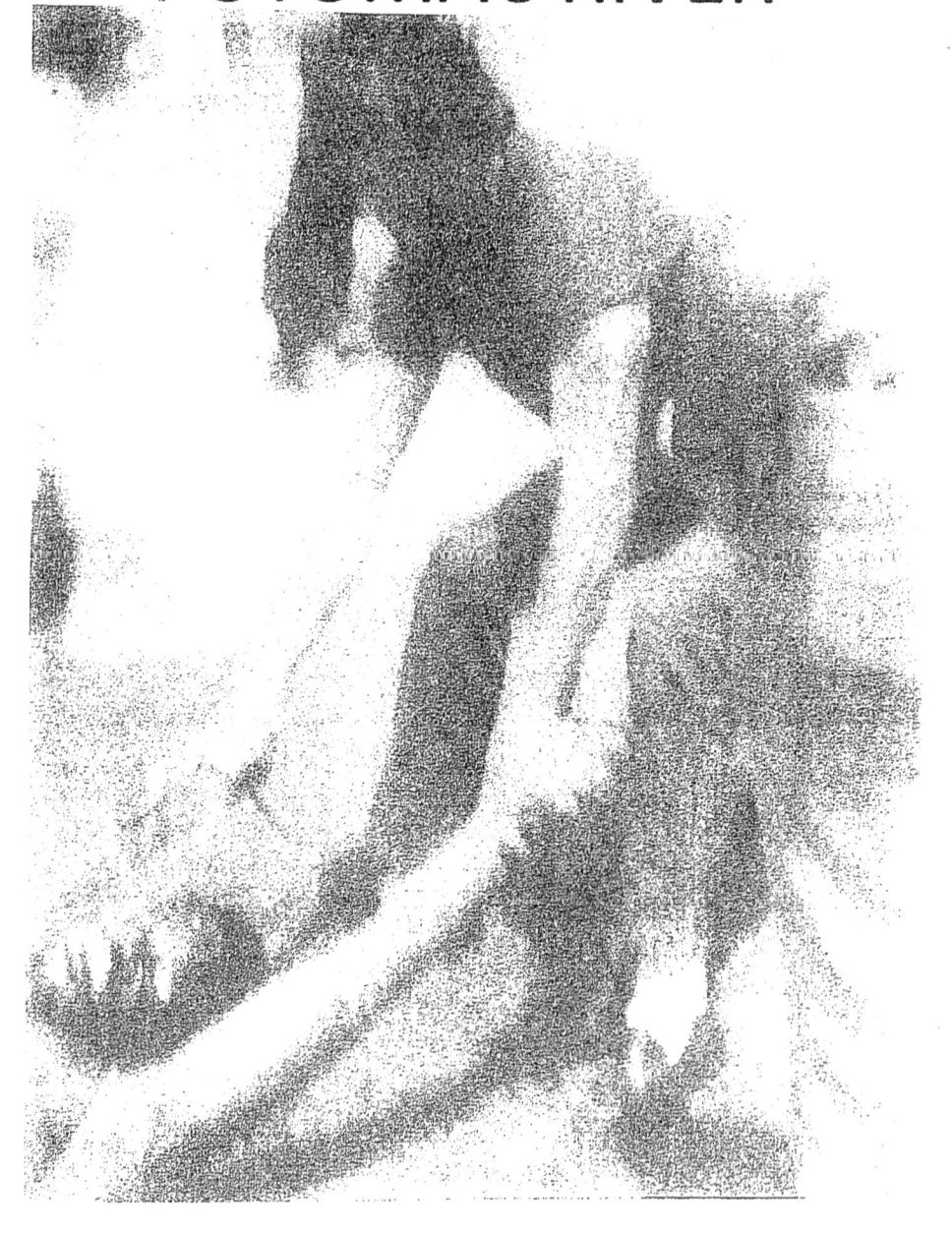

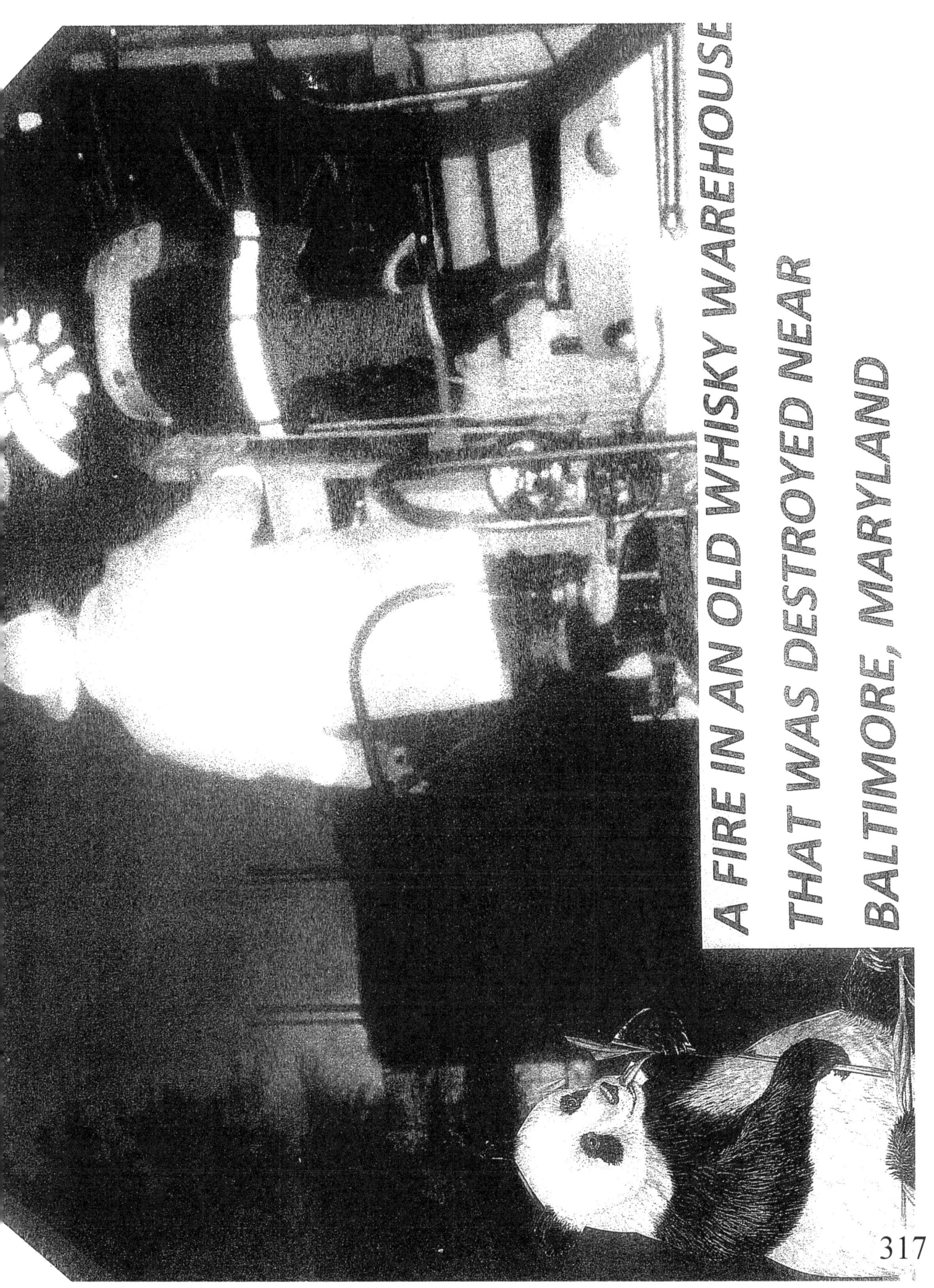

A FIRE IN AN OLD WHISKY WAREHOUSE THAT WAS DESTROYED NEAR BALTIMORE, MARYLAND

A 3 ALARM FIRE DESTROYS A LARGE WAREHOUSE IN WASHINGTON DC

RIVER NEAR THE OLD ANGLER'S INN

A BODY FLOATING IN THE POTOMAC RIVER NEAR THE OLD ANGLERS INN

ON THIS CALL BOBBY GOLLAN AND I MET
THE DC FIRE CHIEF, CHIEF MILLARD SUTTON

7 KILLED

4-Alarm Blaze On Calvert St. Fought 2 Hours

Seven elderly invalids, trapped on the top floor of a nursing home, were burned to death yesterday in one of the most tragic fires in Washington history.

The Mount Vernon Nursing Home, a four-story brick building at 2301 Calvert st. nw, burned for two hours while more than 200 firemen manning 53 pieces of equipment battled the four-alarm blaze.

REST HOME FIRE KILLS SEVEN PERSONS

HE WAS A PRETTY NICE CAT, AND HE LET US STAY THERE AND WATCH THE FIRE

GUYS RIDING RESCUE 3 IN THE BRONX
ABOUT 1980 OR SO

A BUILDING FIRE IN MANHATTAN, NY

THE OLNEY INN BURNS DOWN IN A MULTI-ALARM FIRE THE DAY THAT IT WAS SUPPOSED TO BE SOLD

THE 5 ALARM FIRE AT THE WEAVER HARDWARE STORE IN GEORGETOWN IN WASHINGTON, DC

THE 5 ALARM FIRE AT THE WEAVER HARDWARE

A FIREFIGHTER SURROUNDED BY SOME NEWLY-ARRIVED PANTHERS AT A FIRE IN NEW YORK CITY

Plane Crash on Bucks Elbow Mountain in the Blue Ridge Mountains

26 KILLED AND 1 INJURIED

WOMAN THAT WANDERED AWAY FROM A NURSING HOME AND WAS RUN OVER BY A TRAIN IN DC

GENERAL ALARM FIRE

AT THE HEIGHT OF THE FIRE

ONE OF THREE DEAD CRIMINALS LYING DEAD ON THE GROUND

THEY DIED IN A CAR CHASE BY POLICE WHEN THEIR CAR WRECKED

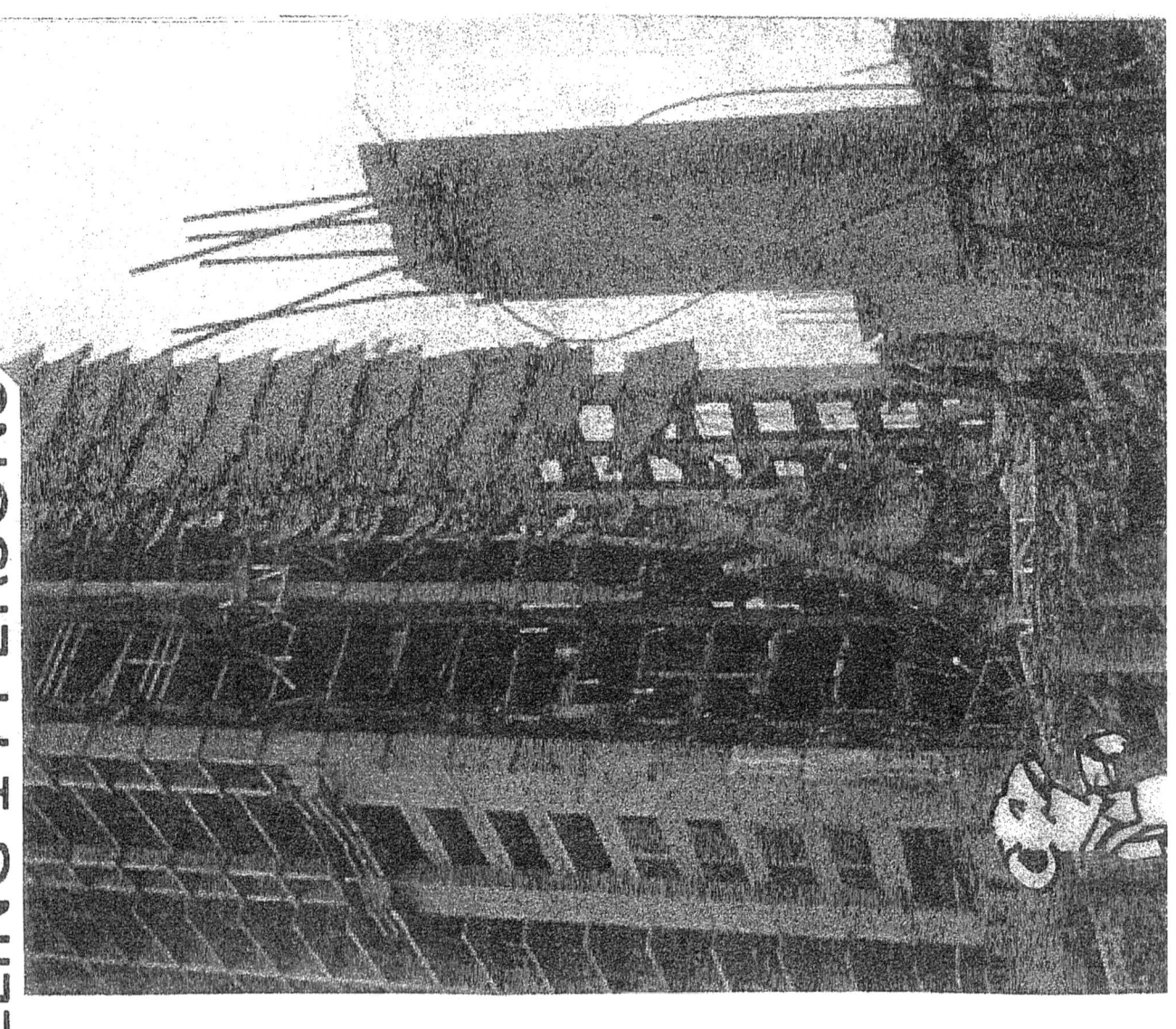

COLLAPSE OF SKYLINE TOWER IN VA KILLING 14 PERSONS

ENGINE CO 82 IN THE SOUTH BRONX
ONE OF THE FEW FIREHOUSES IN THE COUNTRY WITH THAT OLD CASTLE LOOK

BUILDING ON FIRE IN QUEENS, NY

MICE WASHING THEIR PETS AT THE LOCAL CAR WASH

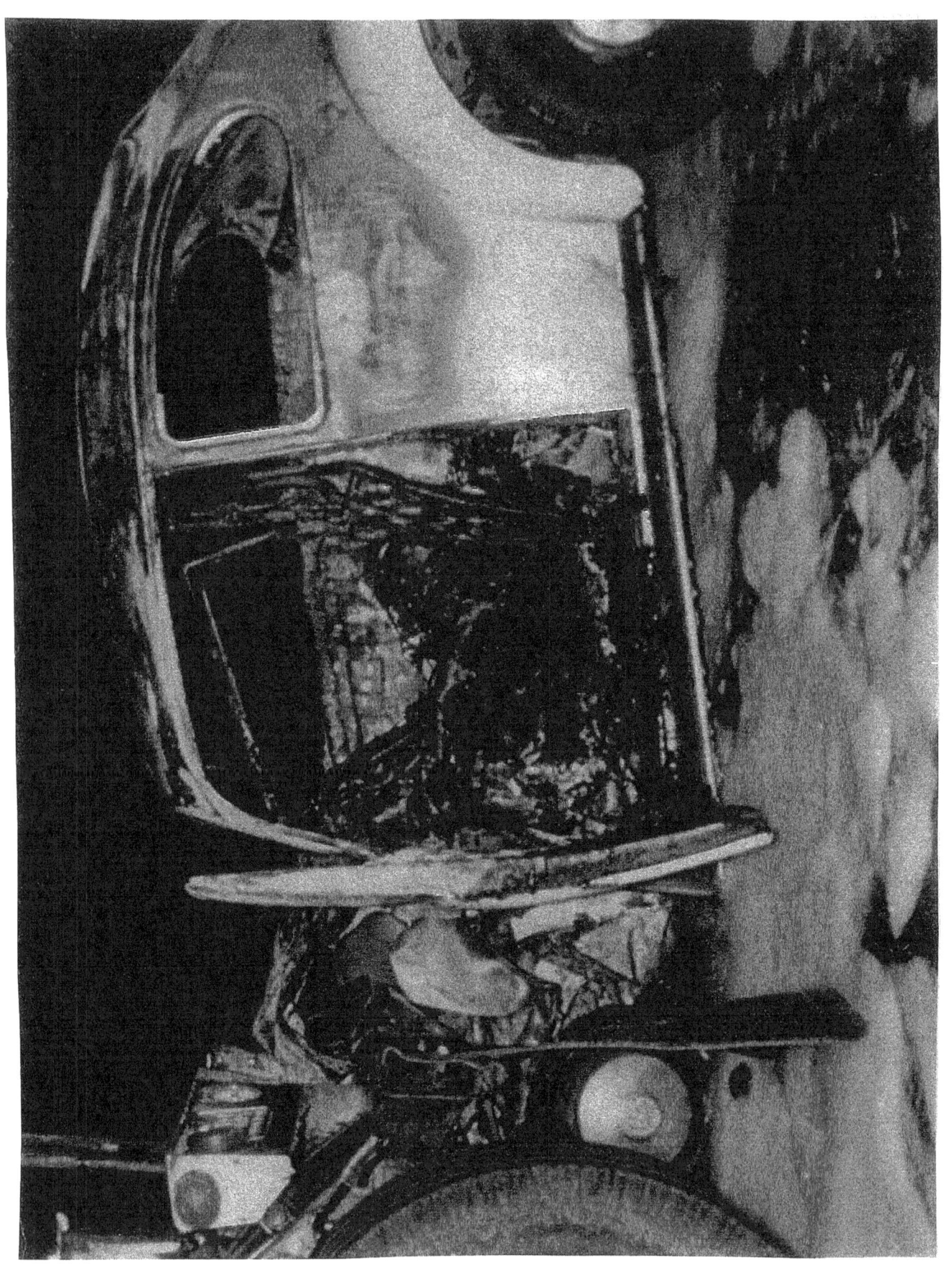

DANNY AT LADDER 124 IN BUSHWICK, BROOKLYN ACE THE MASCOT DOG IN 1980

ACE CHEWING ON A LARGE BONE

A MAJOR FIRE IN THE BRONX, NEW YORK

Three Alarm Fire in D.C.

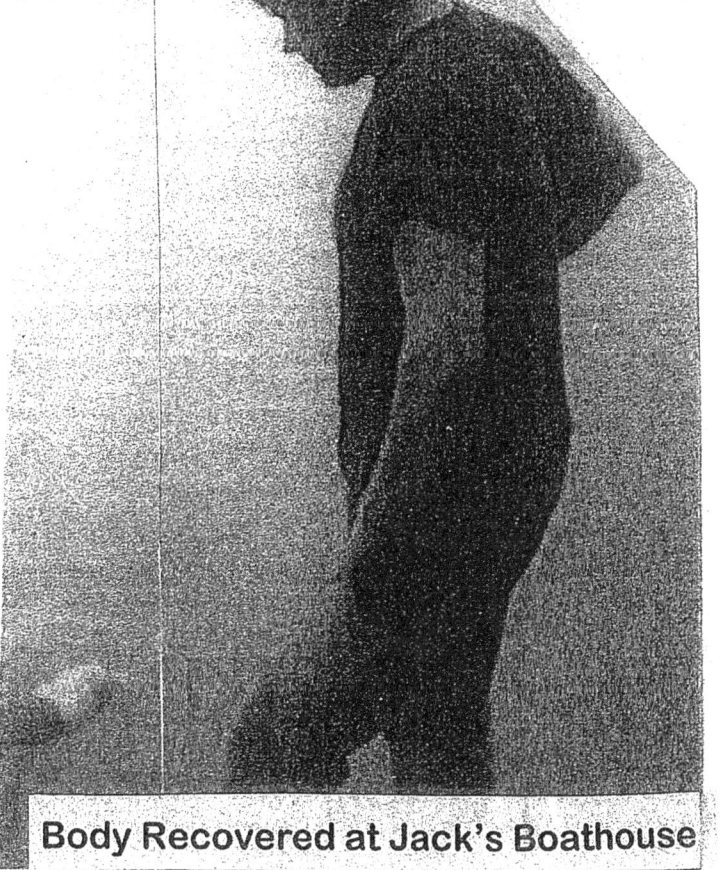

Body Recovered at Jack's Boathouse

FATAL WRECK AND FIRE KILLS TWO VICTIMS ON 270

2 Horses Burned to Death in Upper County MD

FIREFIGHTERS REST ON TOP OF A LOCAL BEAR AS A WAREHOUSE BURNS DOWN BEHIND THEM IN WESTMINSTER, MARYLAND

LARGE FIRE IN THE BRONX

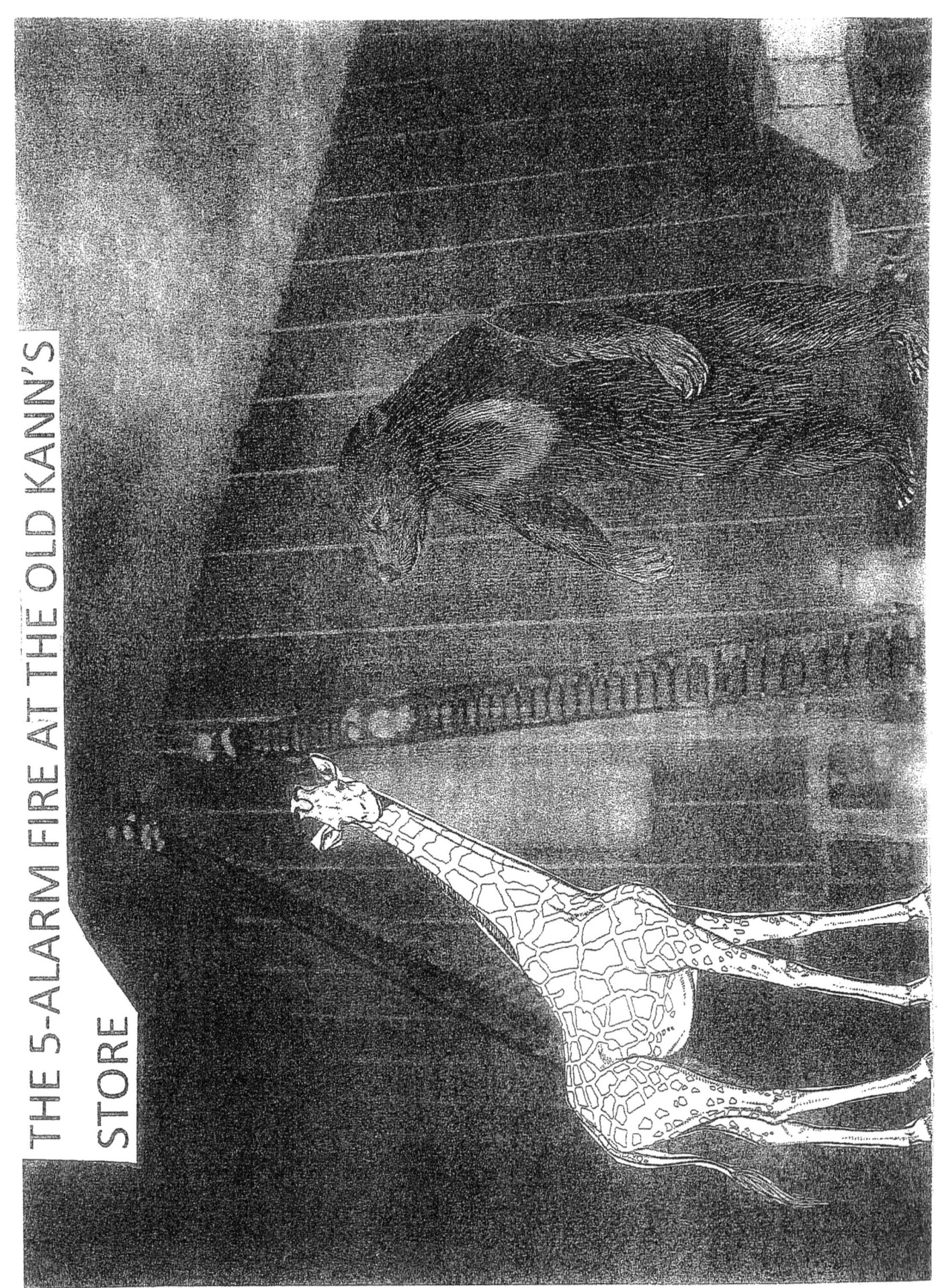

THE 5-ALARM FIRE AT THE OLD KANN'S STORE

A FIRE IN QUEENS, NY

Fatal Plane Crash on the Savage Farm in Gaithersburg, MD

Rescue #2 in Brooklyn, NY Displays on

A Wall Depicting Sections

Of Fences where People Have

Been Impaled after Jumping

ONE OF THE PETS FROM AN ENGINE COMPANY IN BROOKLYN AT A BUILDING ON FIRE

A 5-ALARM FIRE IN THE BRONX NEW YORK

3 FIRE CHIEFS SIZING UP THE SCENE AT A BUILDING FIRE TO DETERMINE THE NEED FOR ANY FIRE FIGHTING

Shopping Center in Gaithersburg, MD Destroyed By Large Fire in Early Morning

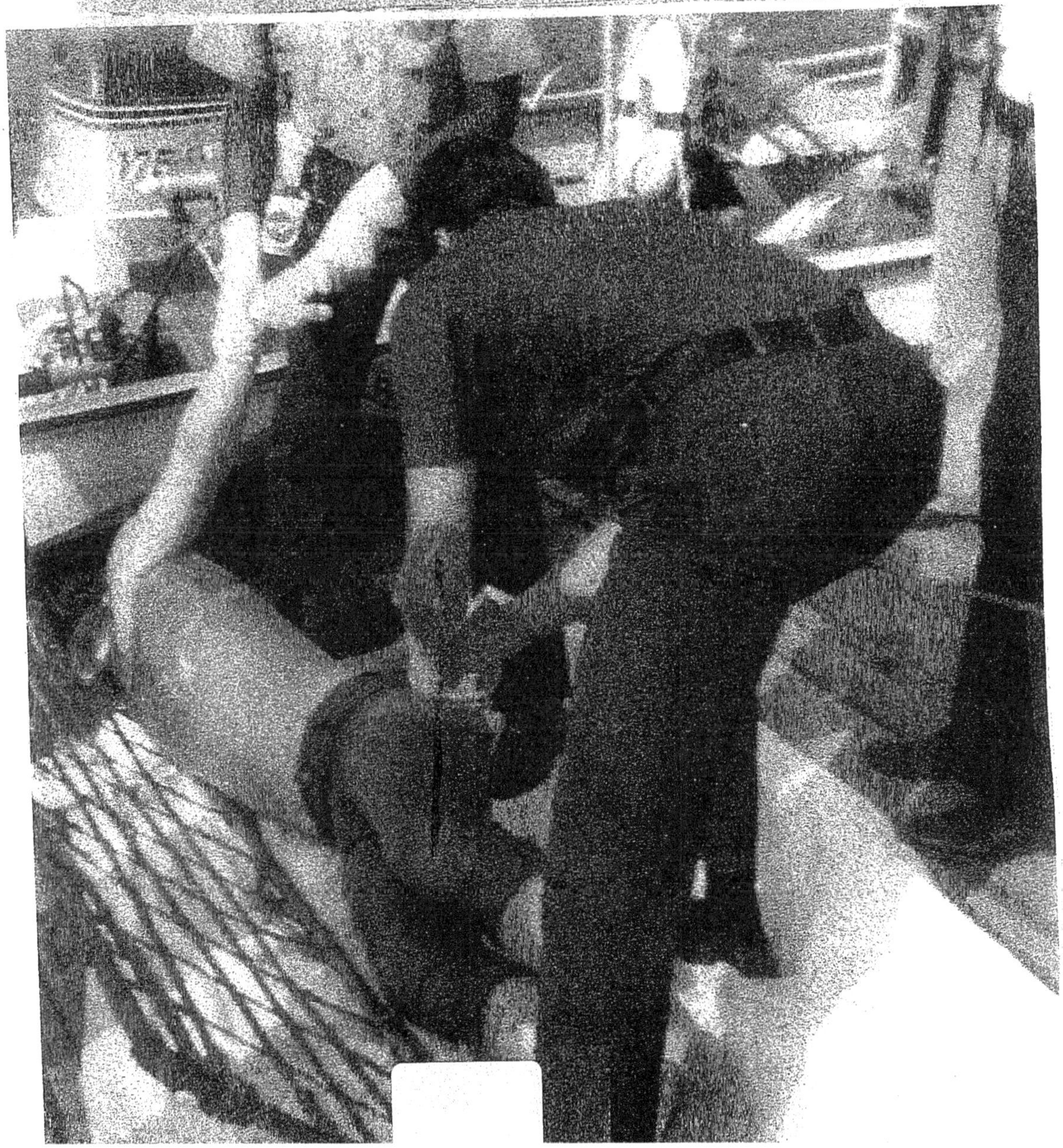

Korvette Department Store in Rockville, MD

Male that Jumped Off a 100 Foot Railroad Trestle

AT LEAST ONE DRIVER IS KILLED WHEN 2 TRUCKS CRASH INTO

Large Fire in Burtonsville, MD

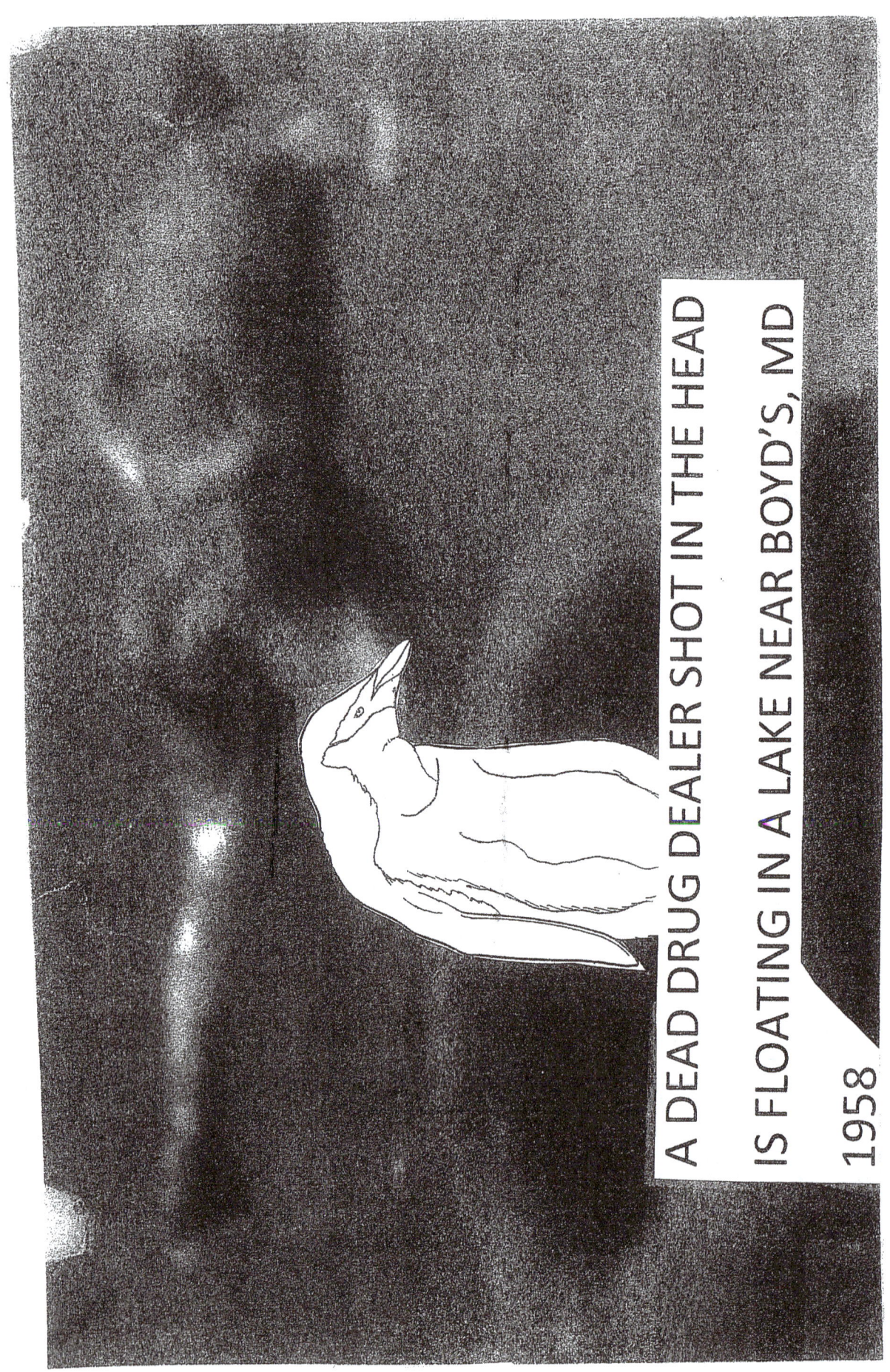

ONE OF THE PETS FROM AN ENGINE COMPANY IN BROOKLYN AT A BUILDING ON FIRE

The Red-Eyed Mustang at the Denver Airport

A FATAL TRUCK WRECK ON ROUTE I-95

A GUY IS CRUSHED TO DEATH UNDER A DIGGING MACHINE IN ROCKVILLE, MD

Fleeing Felon Drowned in the Anacostia River in DC

Fire in the Bronx, NY

357

FIREFIGHTERS IN THE BRONX BATTLING A HUGE FIRE NEAR HUNT'S POINT BY THE EAST RIVER

5-Alarm Oil Fire in the Bronx, NY

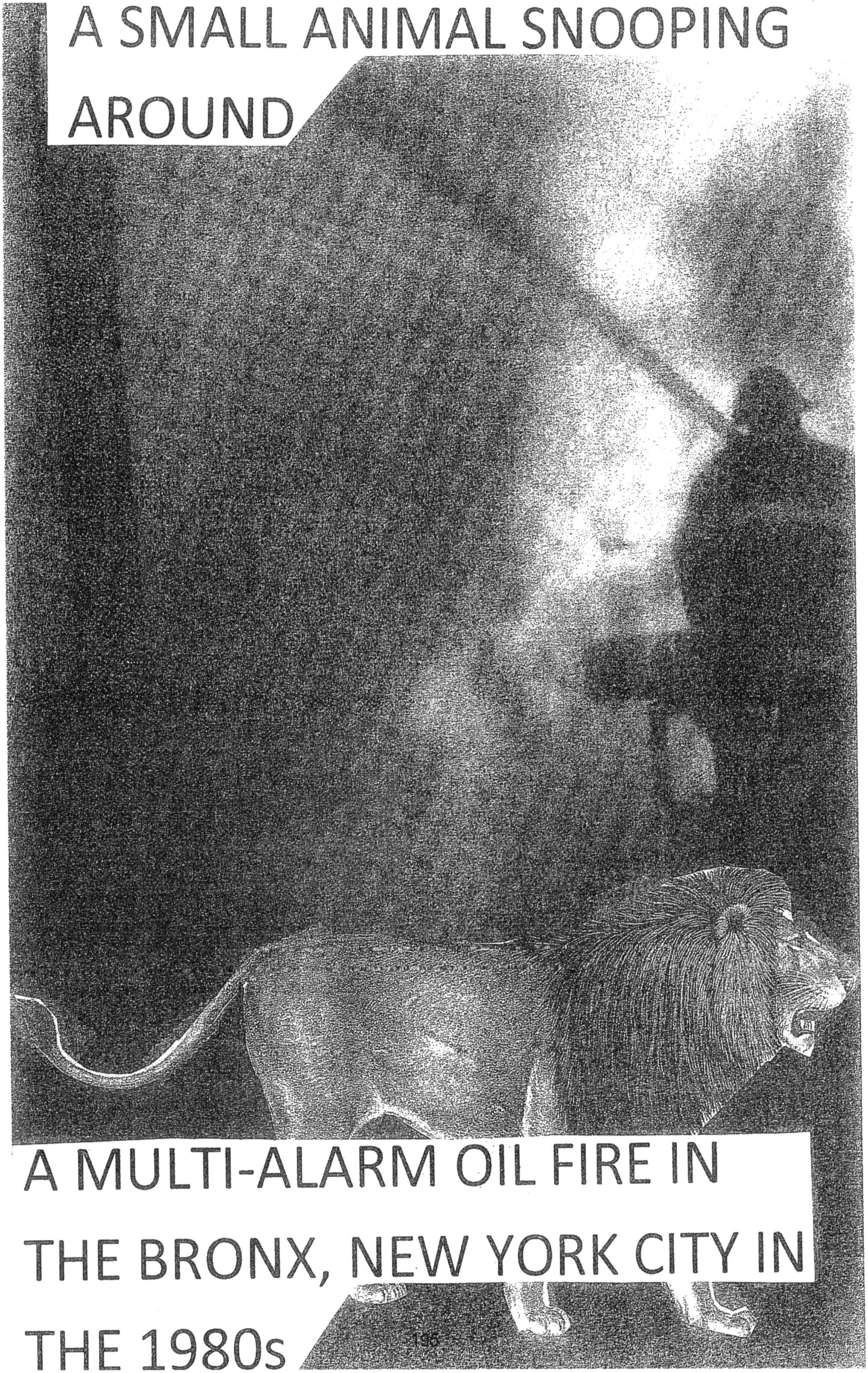

A SMALL ANIMAL SNOOPING AROUND

A MULTI-ALARM OIL FIRE IN THE BRONX, NEW YORK CITY IN THE 1980s

2 GUYS KILLED ON THE GW PARKWAY NEAR THE CABIN JOHN BRIDGE IN VIRGINIA IN THE 1980s

A THIRD-ALARM FIRE IN BETHESDA WHEN A ROW OF STORES BURNED UP IN 1959

DANNY JR AT LUMBERYARD FIRE IN ROCKY MOUNT, NC

2 Buses Collide Near the Mormon Temple In Silver Spring, MD

A GOOD-LOOKING ZEBRA

A TRAIN WRECK IN CHASE, MD THAT KILLED 17 PERSONS

Fatal Wreck

Liberty Mill Fire in Germantown, MD

4-Alarm Blaze Fells 36 Firemen

School Children Write Individual Notes To the 911 Fire Fighters in NY

Dear rescue workers thank you helping America, We are proud of you. Hayden

World Trade Center – After 911

A CHIEF PONDERING THE NEED FOR A RESCUE SQUAD AT THE SCENE OF A FATAL ACCIDENT

BOWIE TRAIN WRECK ABOUT 1962
7 PERSON'S ARE KILLED 100 INJURIED

THIS GUY WAS BURNED SO BAD THAT SOME OF US PRAYED

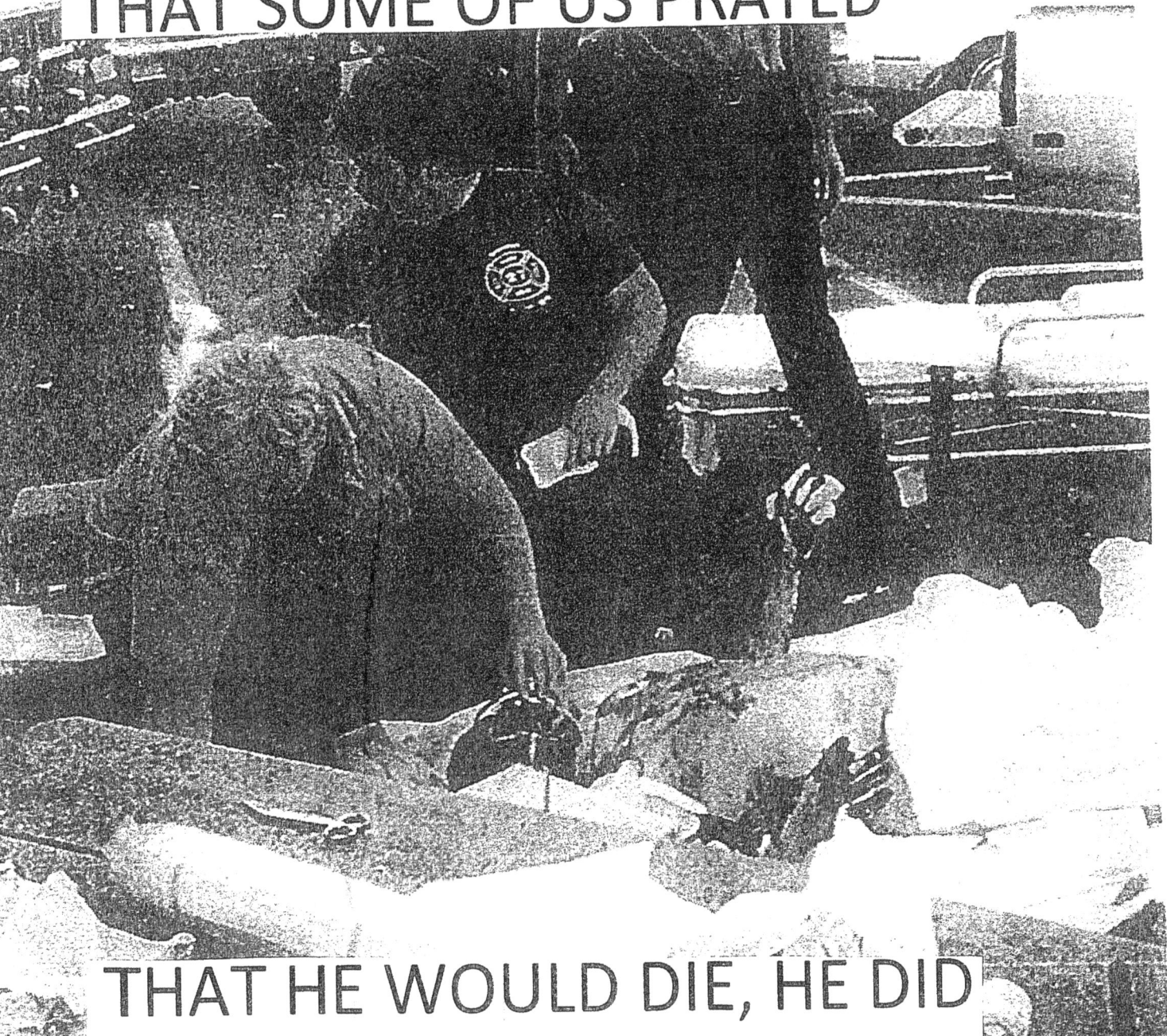

THAT HE WOULD DIE, HE DID BUT IT TOOK ANOTHER 10 HOURS OR SO OF SUFFERING

A PLANE CRASHED INTO A HOUSE IN COLUMBIA, MD KILLING AT LEAST 5 VICTIMS ON THE PLANE

A BAD WRECK IN ROCKVILLE

FATAL HANG GLIDER ACCIDENT IN GERMANTOWN, MD

FIRE DESTROYS AN HISTORIC HOTEL IN GETTYSBURG, PA WHERE PRESIDENT EISENHOWER ONCE SLEPT

SARA RALL AT THE BCCRS HOLDING A BEAR

Recovering Body from Car Near Brighton Dam, MD

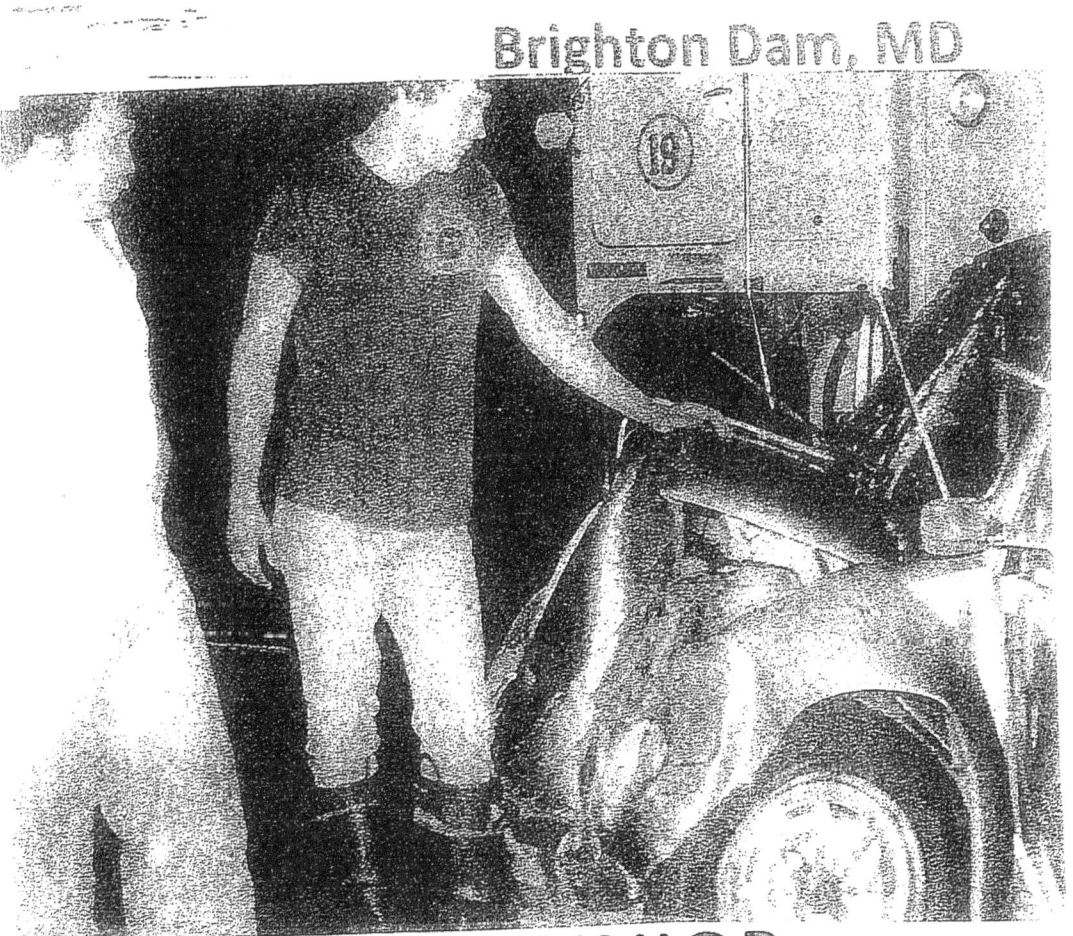

DANNY AND JUNIOR BLACKWOOD AT FATAL WRECK— BODY STILL IN CAR

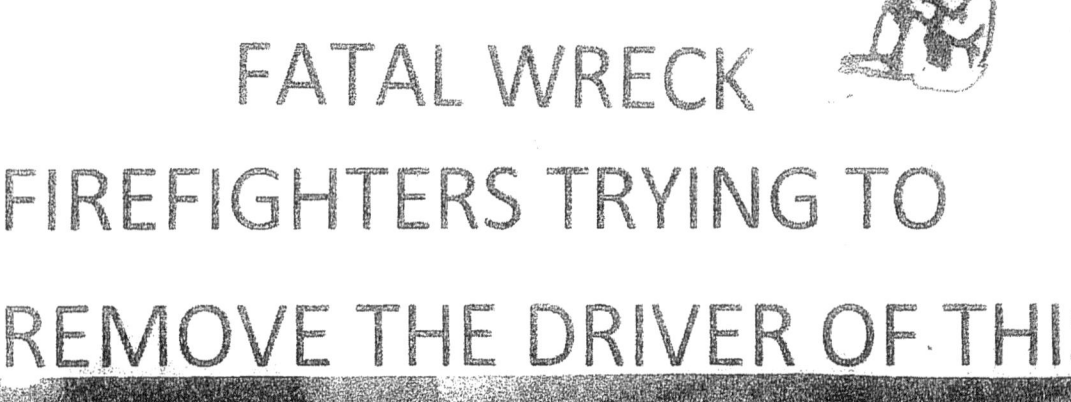

FATAL WRECK FIREFIGHTERS TRYING TO REMOVE THE DRIVER OF THIS OVERTURNED PICKUP TRUCK

GENERAL ALARM FIRE IN MONTGOMERY COUNTY, MARYLAND

FIRE ENGINES IN THE BRONX IN THE 1970s AND 80s

HOUSE FIRE 7 FATALS MOTHER

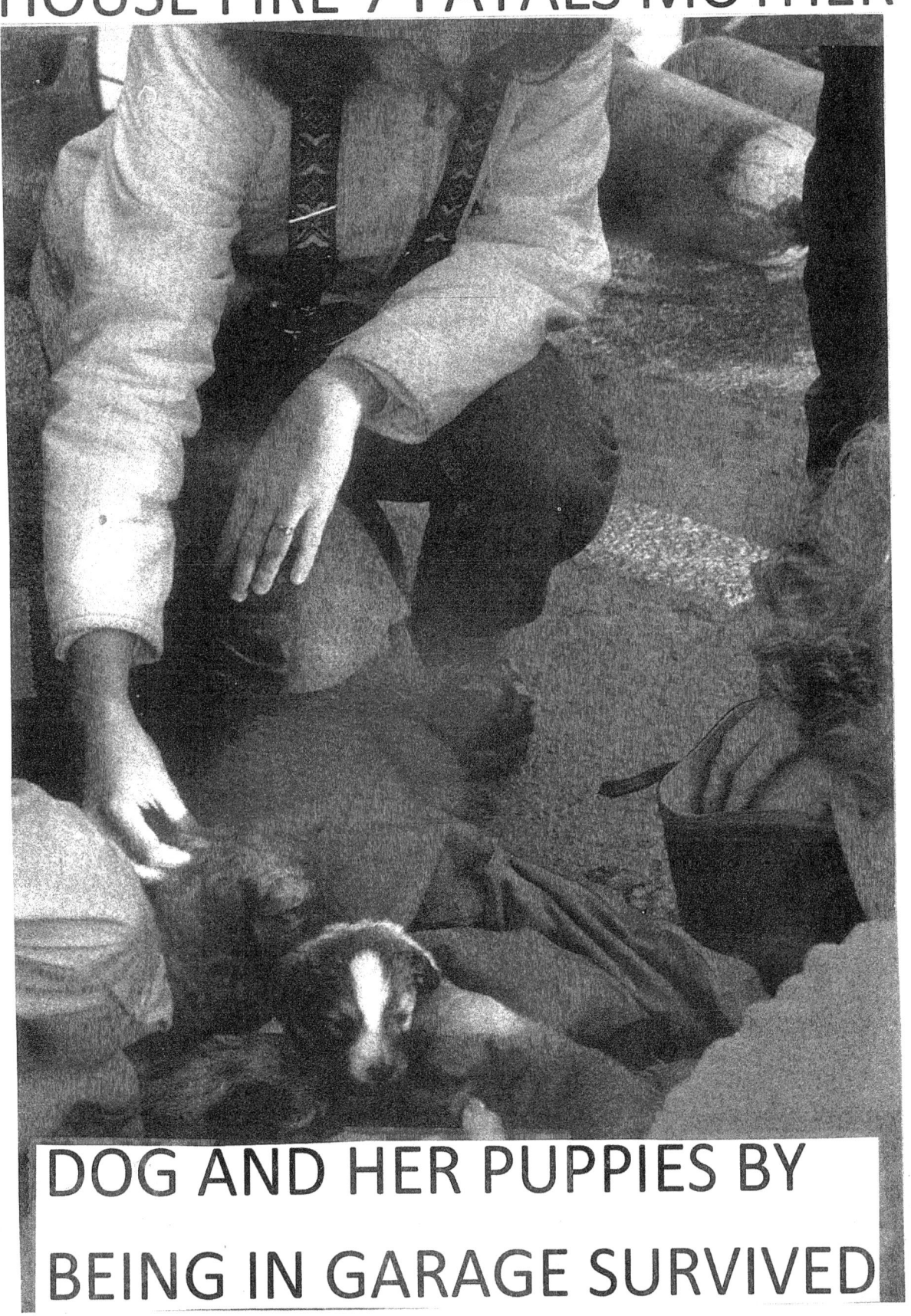

DOG AND HER PUPPIES BY BEING IN GARAGE SURVIVED

AIRPLANE CRASH IN ROCK CREEK PARK IN THE 1950s

AIRPLANE CRASH IN ROCK CREEK PARK IN THE 1950s

384

2 Elderly Ladies Killed on I-270 After Running into a Dump Truck in Rockville, Md.

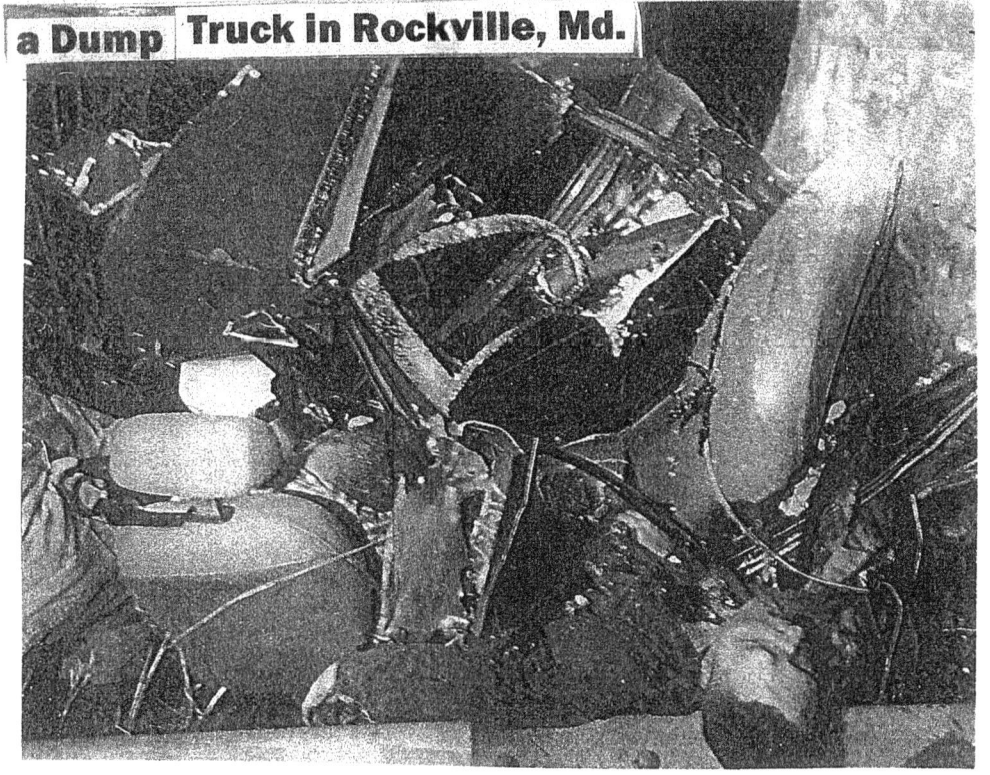

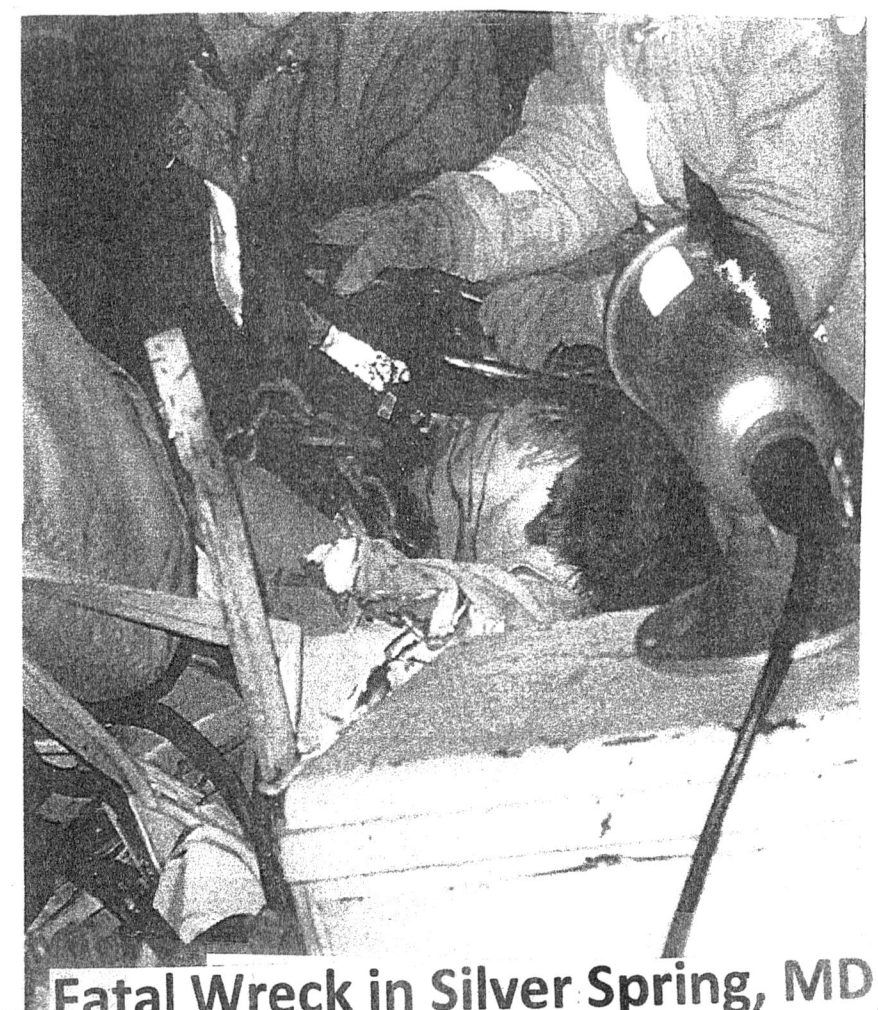

Fatal Wreck in Silver Spring, MD

Plane Crash and Fire at Montgomery Air Park in Gaithersburg, MD

FATAL TRUCK WRECK ON THE BELTWAY NEAR BETHESDA, MD

Retrieving Body from Potomac River in MD

NOTE LARGE PANDA BEAR

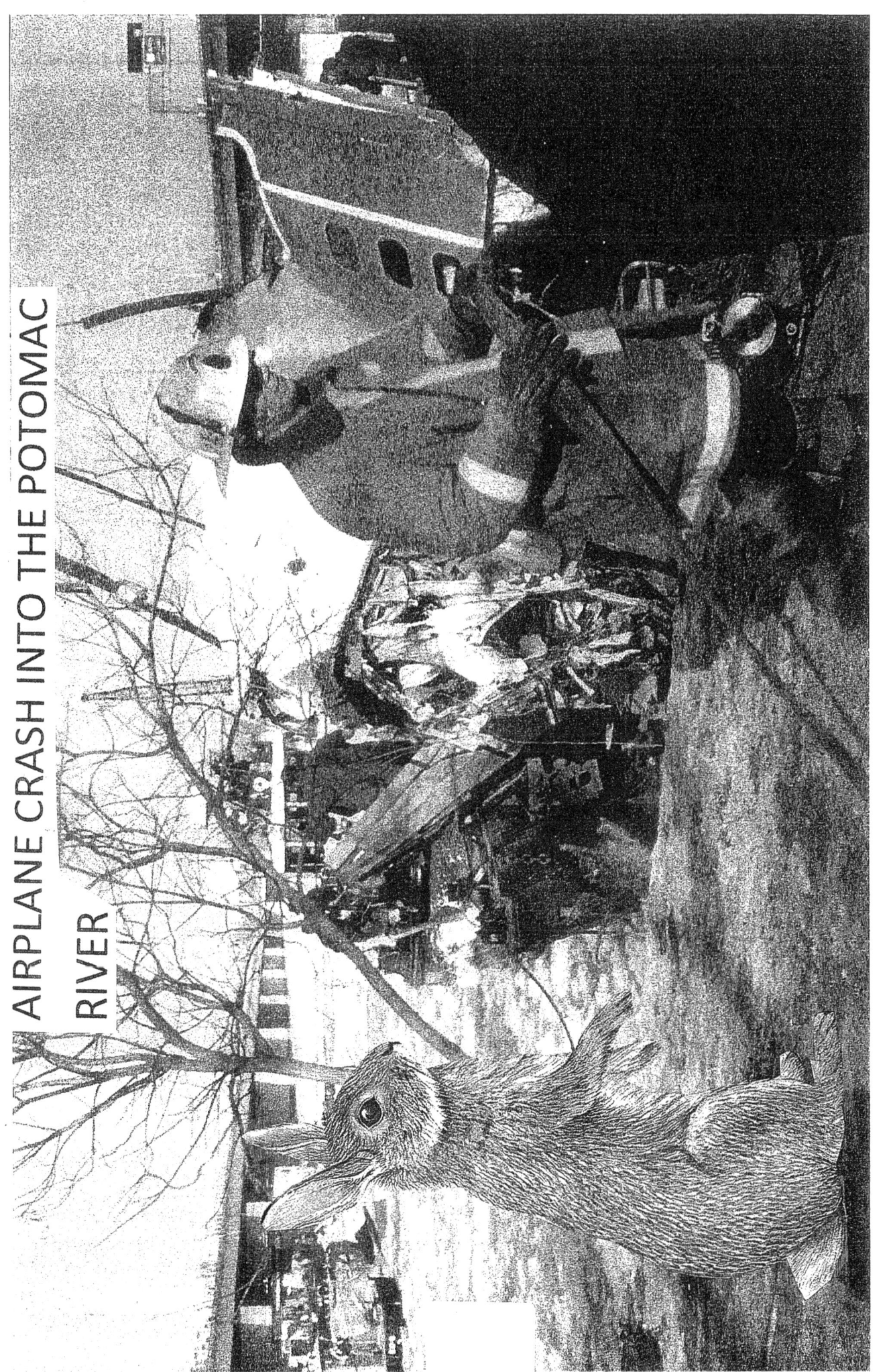

AIRPLANE CRASH INTO THE POTOMAC RIVER

A 5-ALARM FIRE IN THE BRONX

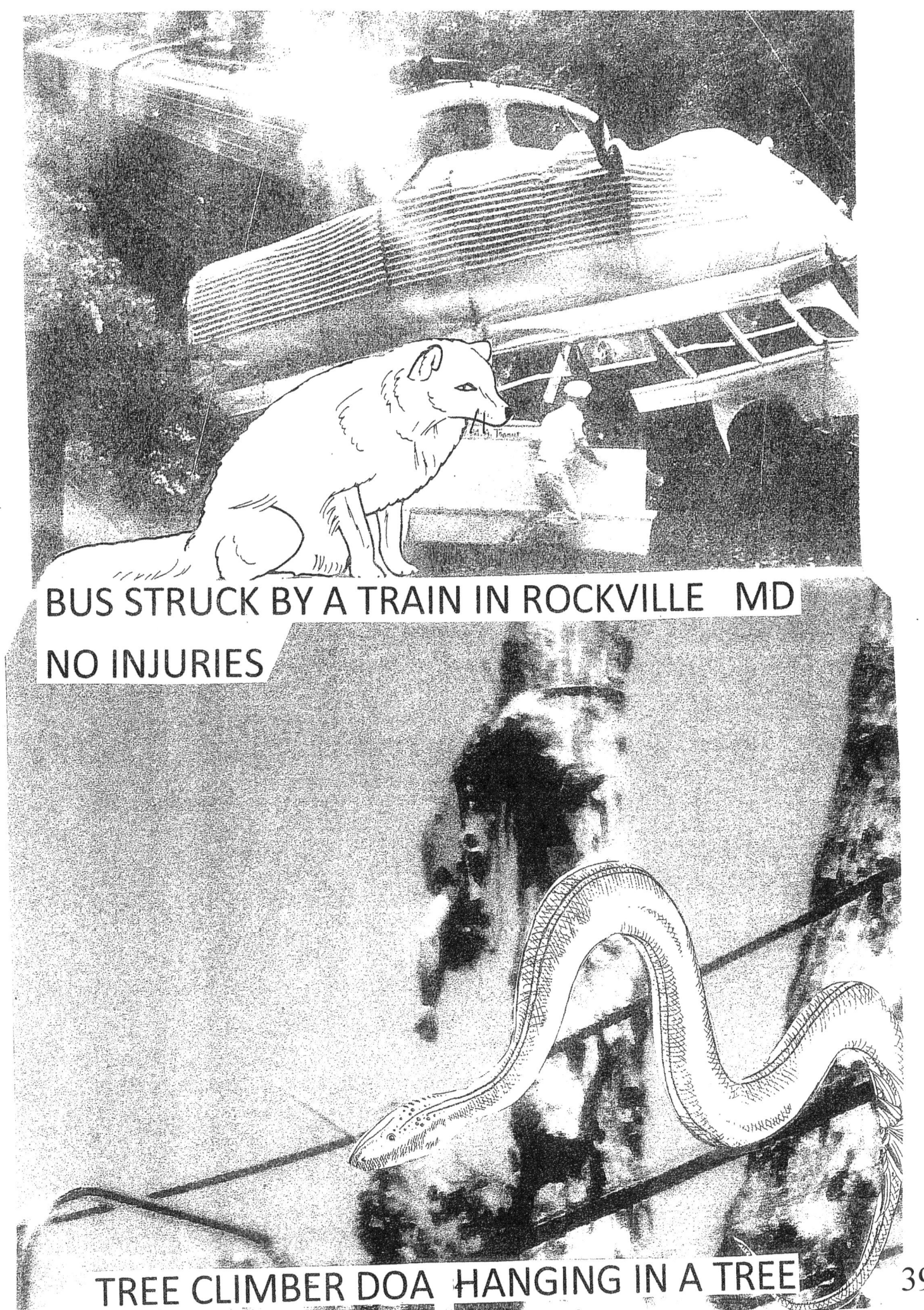

LARGE FIRE IN THE BRONX BY THE HELLGATE BRIDGE KILLING SEVERAL VICTIMS

LARGE FIRE IN THE BRONX BY THE HELLGATE BRIDGE IN THE 1980s KILLING SEVERAL VICTIMS

The Desperate Hours

LARGE FIRE IN THE BRONX BY THE HELLGATE BRIDGE IN THE 1980s KILLING SEVERAL VICTIMS

FATAL TRUCK WRECK ON THE CABIN JOHN BRIDGE

THIS WOMAN WAS RUN OVER BY A TRAIN

A LARGE FIRE IN OWENS MILLS, MD WHEN A 6-STORY OLD WHISKEY DISTILLERY WAREHOUSE BURNS DOWN

2 HORSES BURN TO DEATH WHEN HORSE TRAILER OVERTURNS IN BARNESVILLE, MD

A DEAD BURNED BODY LIES IN HIS CAR AFTER RUNNING INTO A GASOLINE TANKER TRUCK ON I-95 CAUSING THE CAR TO EXPLODE

A MOTEL IN GAITHERSBURG, MD WHERE THE WASHINGTON REDSKINS FOOTBALL TEAM ONCE STAYED AND TRAINED AT BURNS DOWN IN THE 1970s

A LARGE SNAKE APPEARING ON THE FIREGROUND

A VERY FAMOUS PAINTING OF THE SISTER SHIP OF THE TITANIC THAT SANK SO LONG AGO

A LARGE DRUG STORE THE SIZE OF A CITY BLOCK IS DESTROYED BY FIRE

NOTICE THE ICE CYCLES ON THE FIRE TRUCK

MY KIDS DEANA AND DANNY JR AT THE LIBERTY MILL FIRE IN 1972 (I AM ON CRUTCHES BECAUSE I HAD RECENTLY BEEN RUN OVER BY A 2-TON TRUCK SUMMER OF 1972 IN A 4-ALARM FIRE 1972 IN GERMANTOWN, MD AND WAS STILL HEALING FROM SOME BROKEN BONES

THE LIBERTY MILL BEFORE IT BURNED DOWN IN 1972

RECOVERING A BODY FROM THE POTOMAC RIVER IN CABIN JOHN, MD

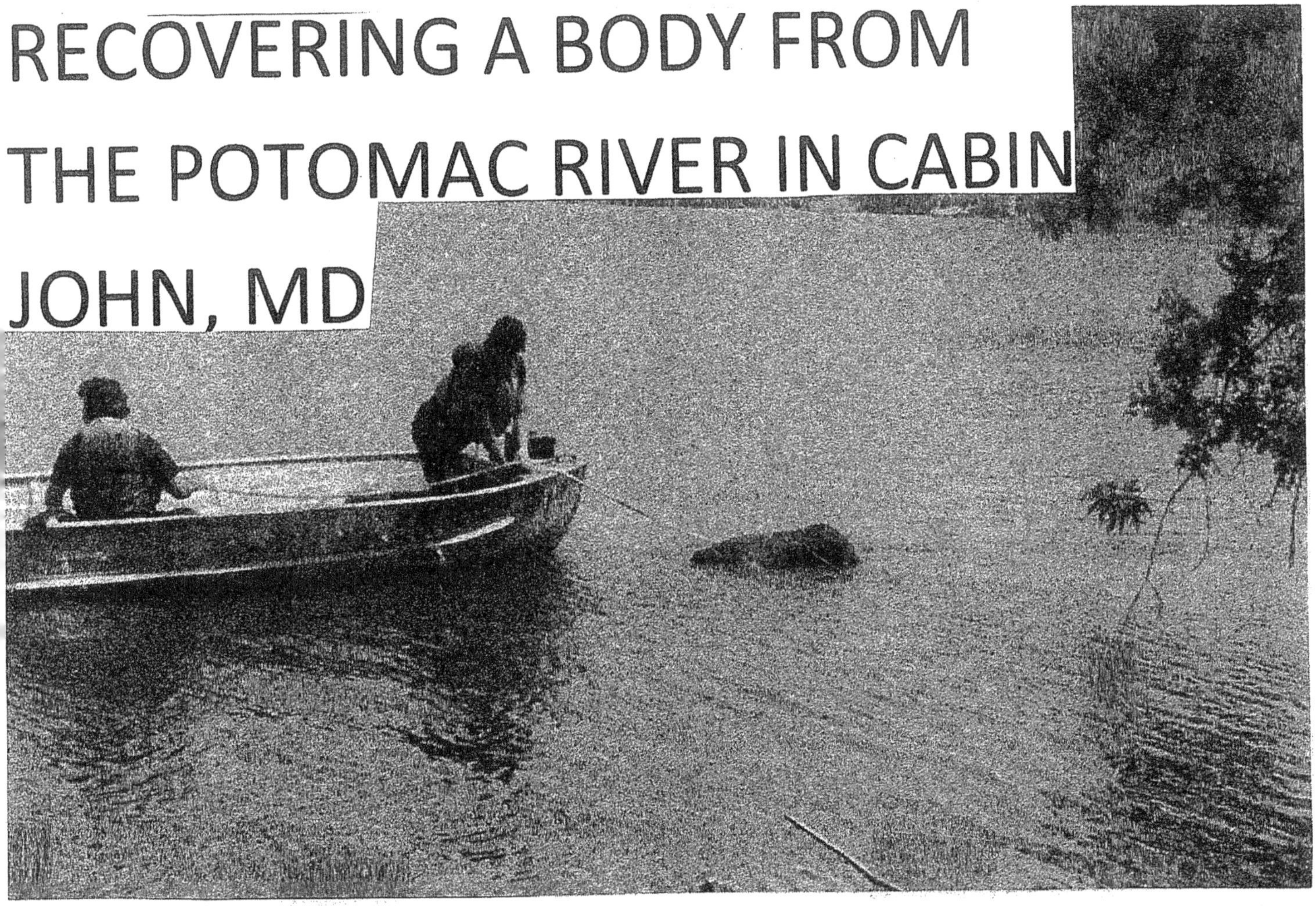

FATAL WRECK IN BETHESDA, MD

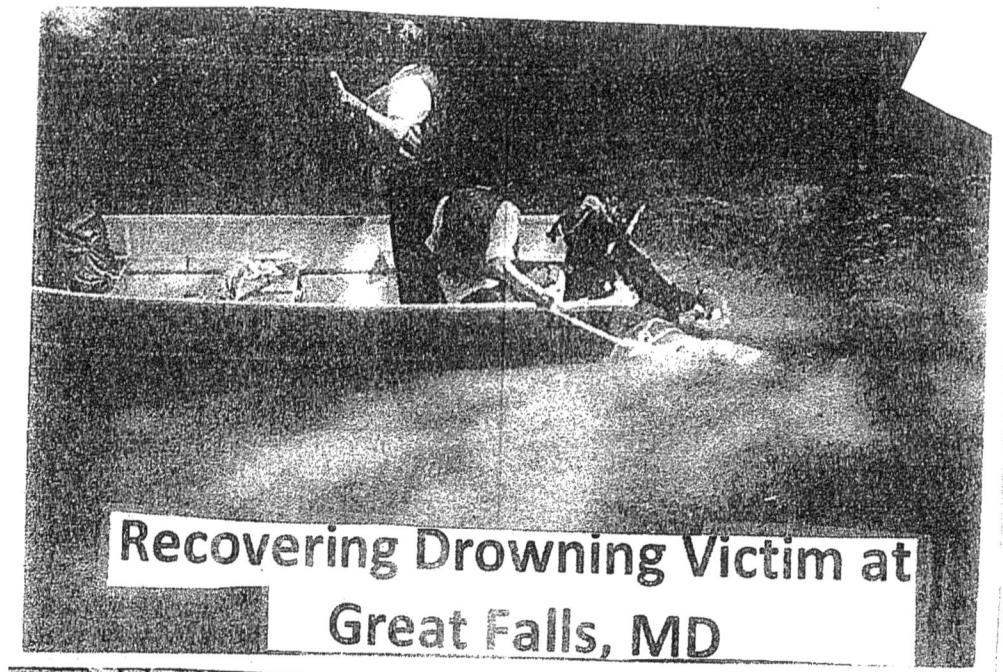

Recovering Drowning Victim at Great Falls, MD

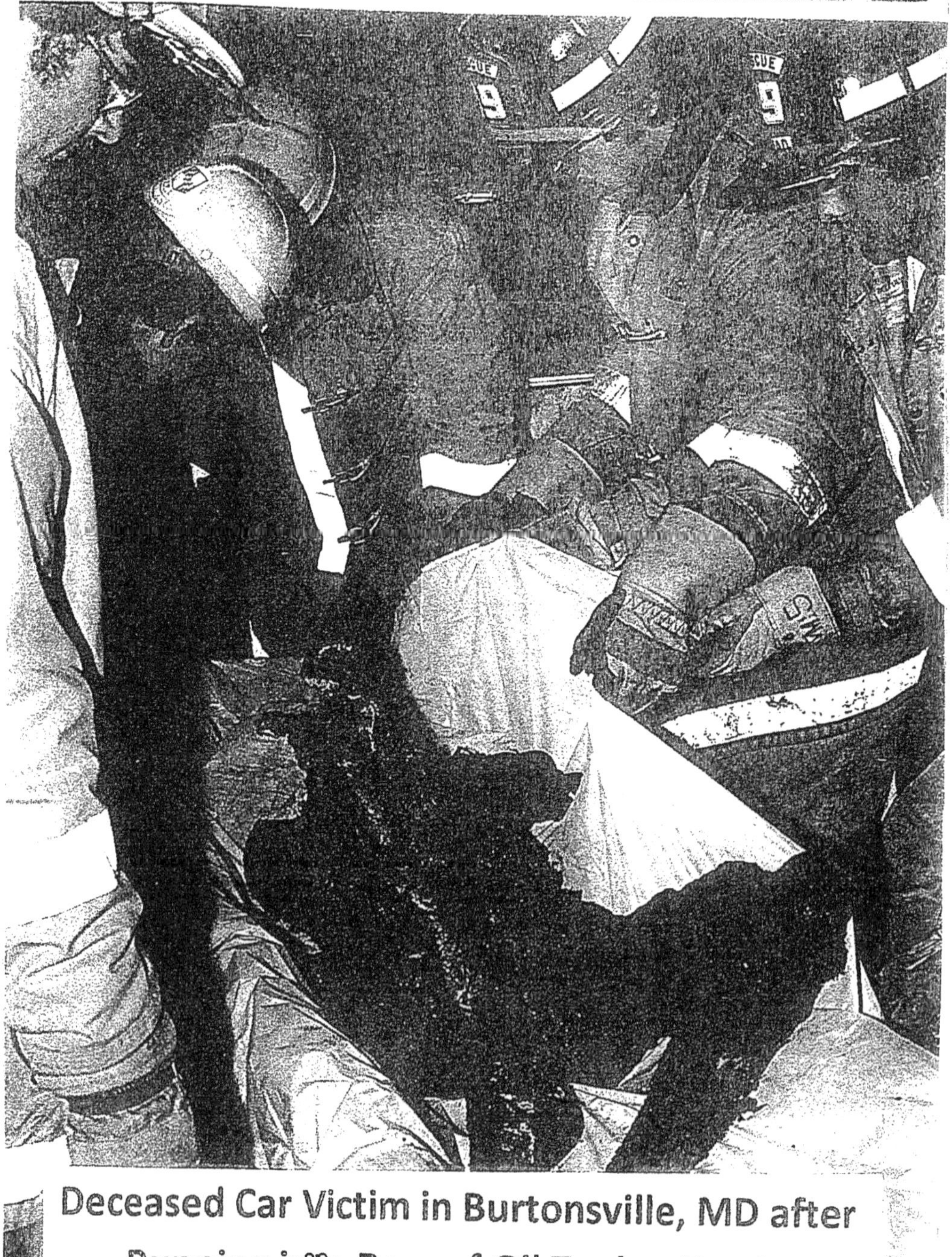

Deceased Car Victim in Burtonsville, MD after Running into Rear of Oil Tanker Truck

Airplane Crash and Fire at the Montgomery Air Park in Gaithersburg, MD

CRASH KILLS PILOT

FATHER OF A FRIEND OF MY SON KILLED WHEN HE TOOK OFF FROM HIS PRIVATE AIRPORT NEAR URBANA, MD

Jersey homes charred

2 PLANES COLLIDED AND FELL INTO SPECTACULAR BALL OF FIRE ONTO TWO SECTIONS OF BERGEN COUNTY ACROSS THE HUDSON RIVER FROM NY

A TOWNHOUSE IN GAITHERSBURG, MD WAS BLOWN DOWN IN A SEVERE WIND STORM

5 Killed on I-95 Wreck in Springfield, VA

5 Killed in Wreck between a Large Dump Truck and Numerous Cars in Springfield, Virginia

RECOVERING A BODY AT GREAT FALLS, MD

FATAL JEEP WRECK ON I-495

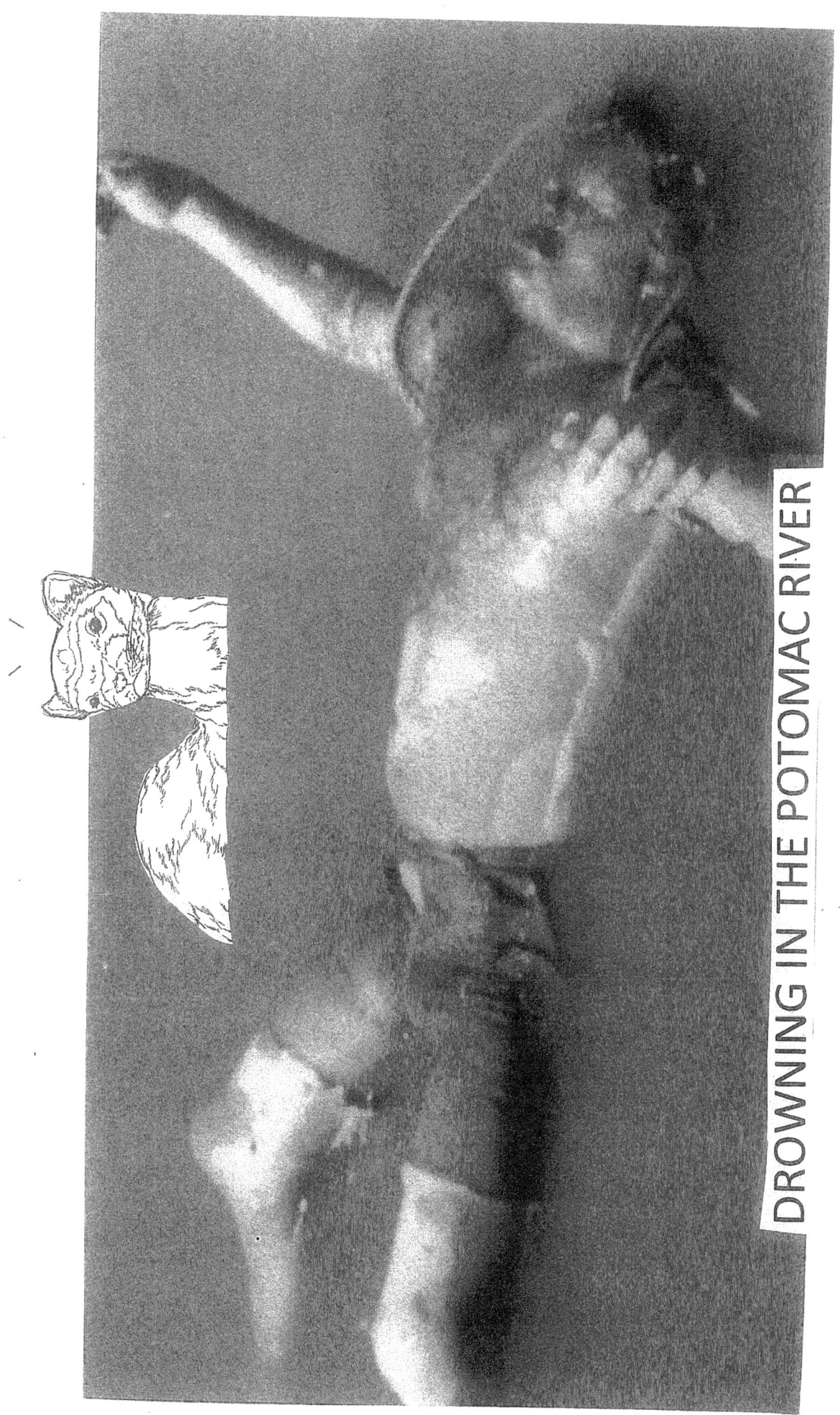

DROWNING IN THE POTOMAC RIVER

RECOVERING A BODY FROM THE POTOMAC RIVER

FATAL WRECK AT THE CABIN JOHN BRIDGE WHEN A TRACTOR TRAILED WENT OVER THE SIDE INTO THE POTOMAC RIVER-THE BODY WAS RAISED UP ONTO THE BRIDGE

BUILDING ON FIRE IN THE BRONX

FIREFIGHTER ED DROOL THE 2ND TAKING IN NIAGARA FALLS

NIAGARA FALLS, YEARS AGO THE ELDERLY BUCK WENT OVER THE AMERICAN FALLS IN AN ICE CHEST AND DIDN'T GIVE A DAM

PASAGE TO THE EARTH'S SURFACE BOOK

Picture this: A group of mice are inside the Grand Canyon. In 1956 there is a deadly collision overhead between 2 commercial airliners, and the mice assisted at the site of the crash until human rescuers could reach the scene the next day. Unfortunately there were no survivors of 128 persons in what was the worst loss of life up to that time. The mice religiously patrolled the disaster area and kept wild animals and snakes at bay and later, as a reward for their service, the mice received a Presidential Declaration for a guided tour of America, nationwide, lasting for however long it takes and with money being no object. It was signed by the President, who also added the words: "from a friendly and loving nation." After the presentation, the mice turned to leave and heard the President say to all as he wiped the tears away: "These little guys are good guys, don't ever forget it, please, you dig."

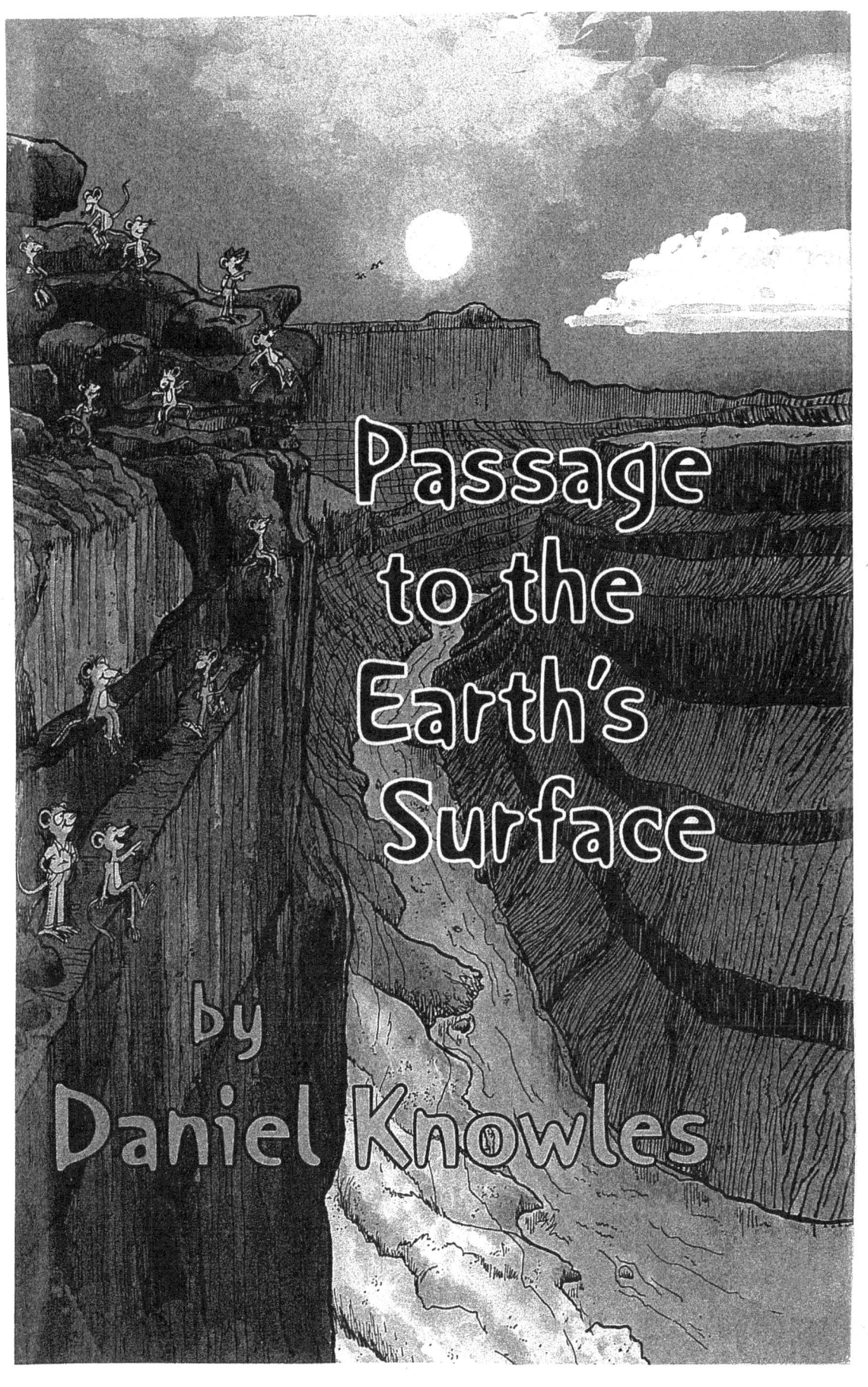

FATAL TRUCK WRECK ON I-95 IN MD

HUNDREDS OF TOURISTS PLACES TO VISIT

TRAVELING ACROSS AMERICA BOOK

FATAL WRECK IN BETHESDA, MD

Paul Bunyon and Babe the Blue Ox
Klamath, California

ONE OF THE GUY'S LOOKING AT THE STATUE OF LIBERTY

A BOX OF ORANGES ON THE SIDE OF THE ROAD IN FRAZEYBURG, OHIO

THE WORLD'S LARGEST TOTEM POLE IN FOYLE, OKL

433

DEVIL'S ROPE MUSEUM

GUY'S GETTING READY TO GAMBLE ON A CASINO BOAT

QUEEN MARY IN LONG BEACH, CA

A MOUSE RUNNING WITH A SMALL BEAR

IN THE ROCKY MOUNTAINS SOME ANTS TEND TO BE SLIGHTLY LARGER THAN THE AVERAGE HOUSEHOLD ANT

SOME OF THE GUYS AT THE OLD WATERING HOLE

Soo Locks and the International Bridge

LONDON BRIDGE

GUY'S TRAVELING TO AND FROM FIREHOUSES BY TRAINS

THE AHWAHNEE HOTEL, YOSEMITE NATIONAL PARK, CA

GUYS POLISHING ROCKS AT THE FIREHOUSE

A SPECIAL PIECE OF FIRE EQUIPMENT TO ATTACK FIRES FROM THE AIR

445

THE FOUR CORNERS' MONUMENT

TOMBSTONE

Tombstone's best preserved historic landmark, retaining its original fixtures & furnishings of 1880. Miners, crafty gamblers and feared gunmen were entertained by the ladies of the night and the bawdiest shows in the west.

OUT WEST

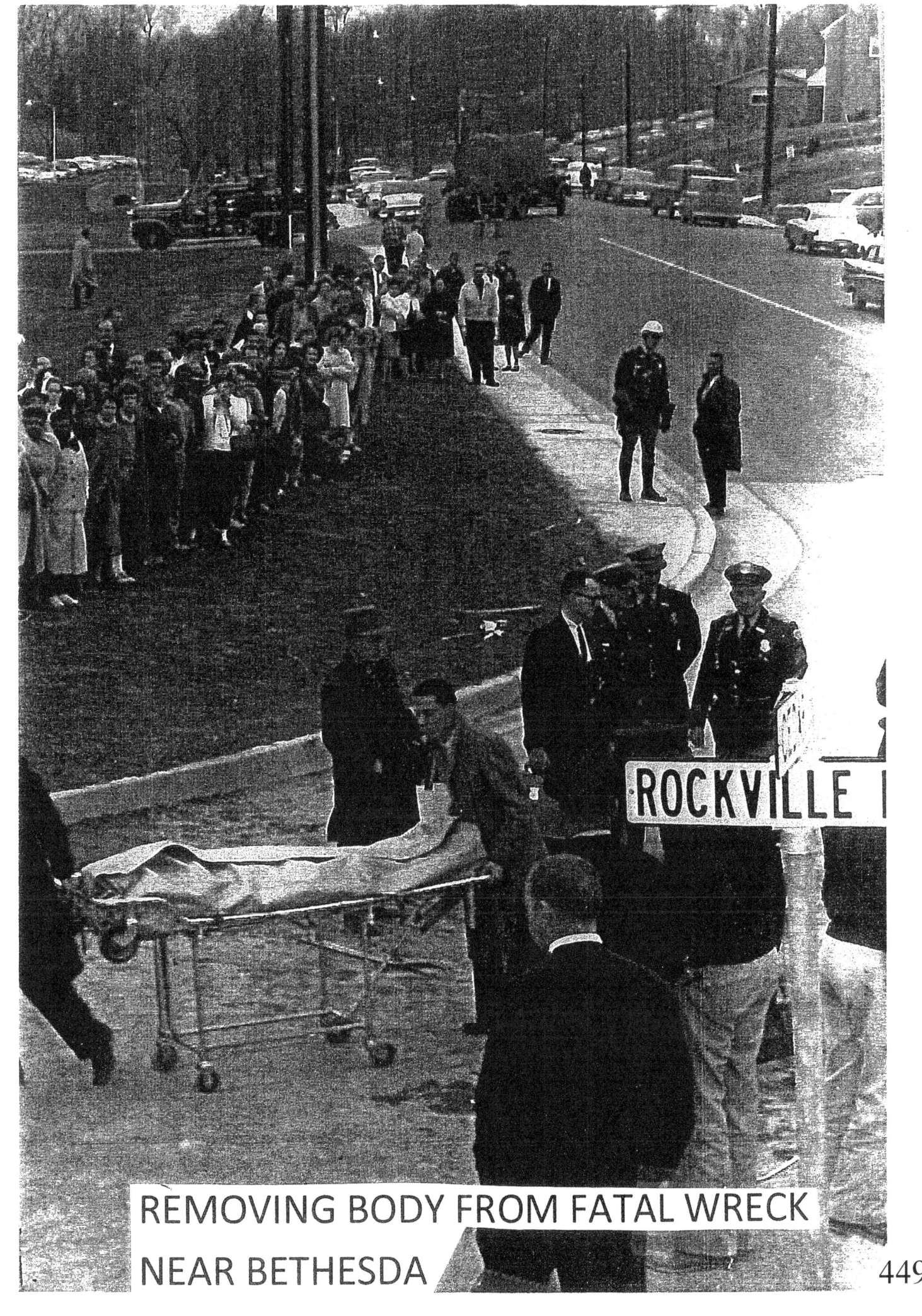

REMOVING BODY FROM FATAL WRECK NEAR BETHESDA

449

FIREFIGHTER'S PERFORMING PART TIME JOBS MOVING COAL TO VARIOUS FIREHOUSES

MOVING ANIMALS ON THE RAIL

IN ARIZONA OFF I-40

MAMMY'S CUPBOARD ON HWY 61 NEAR ST. FRANCISVILLE, LA

454

A GUY IS CRUSHED TO DEATH UNDER A DIGGING MACHINE IN ROCKVILLE, MD

A LARGE FIRE IN THE BRONX

CATS FROM THE RESCUE SQUAD
1970s

DANNY AND BILLY FITZGERALD AT JACK'S BOATHOUSE WITH SEVERAL RECOVERED BODIES FROM THE POTOMAC RIVER IN MD

THE WORLD'S LARGEST HOLSTEIN SALEM SUE IN NORTH DAKOTA

BUFFALO BILL HISTORICAL CENTER, CODY, WY

THE WORLD'S LARGEST BUFFALO IN JAMESTOWN, NORTH DAKOTA

"Slowin' Down To Take A Look"

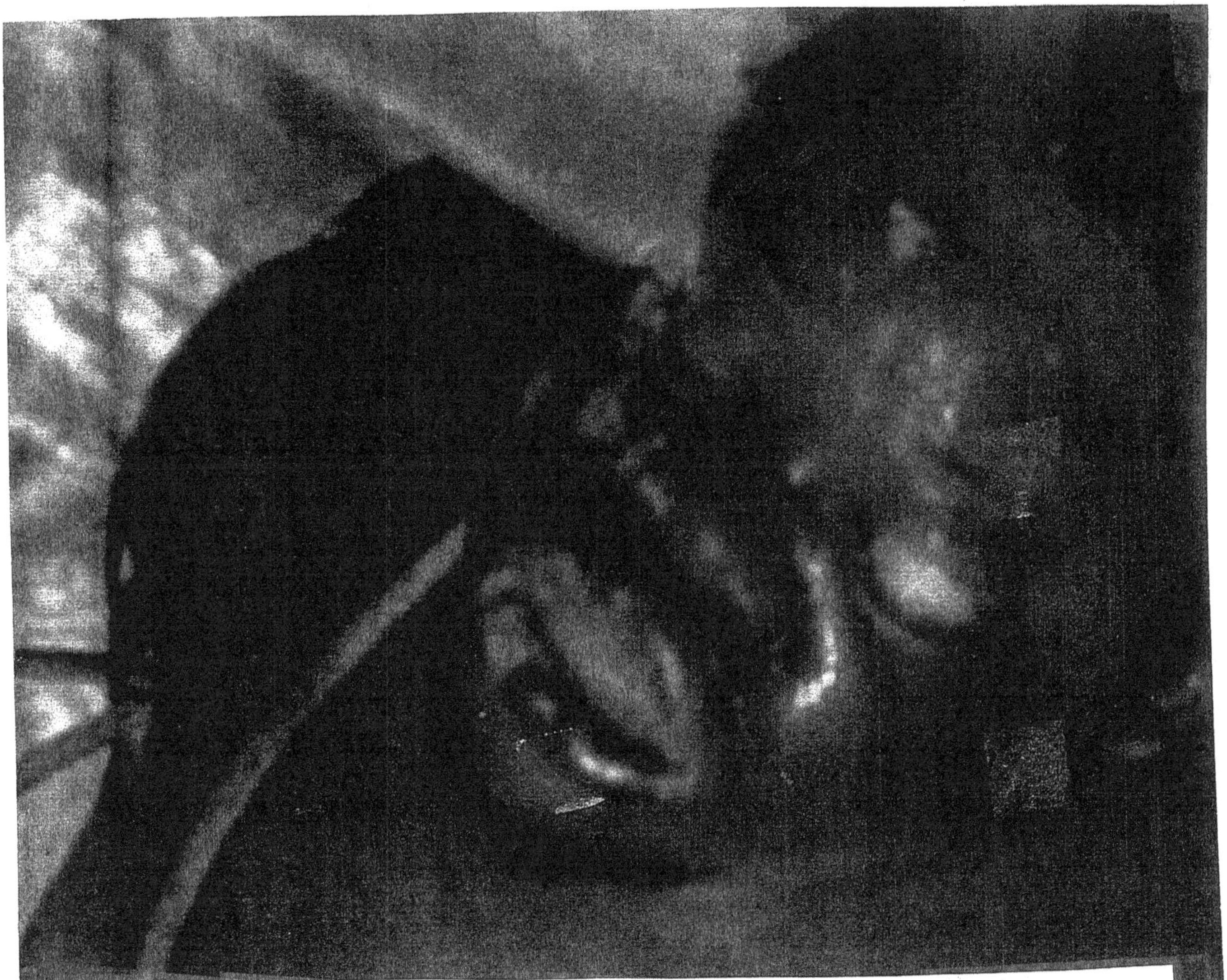

THIS GUY DROWNED AND WAS RECOVERED

Building Fire in Bushwick, Brooklyn, NY

World's Largest McDonald's®
I-44 Vinita, Oklahoma

A BODY AFTER BEING TOWED IN BY BOAT IN THE POTOMAC RIVER

A TRUCK RUNS INTO A BUILDING KILLING THE DRIVER IN UPPER MARLBORO, MD

THE WASHINGTONIAN MOTEL IN GAITHERSBURG, MD IS DESTROYED IN A 4-ALARM FIRE IN THE 1970s

AT A 4-ALARM FIRE WHERE A TRAIN CAME BY AND SLICED 3 HOSELINES ACROSS THE RR TRACKS

BUILDING DESTROYED IN A 2-ALARM FIRE IN TAKOMA PARK, MD

Old Longfellow School Gutted by Fire

2 Killed on I-270 in Urbana, MD

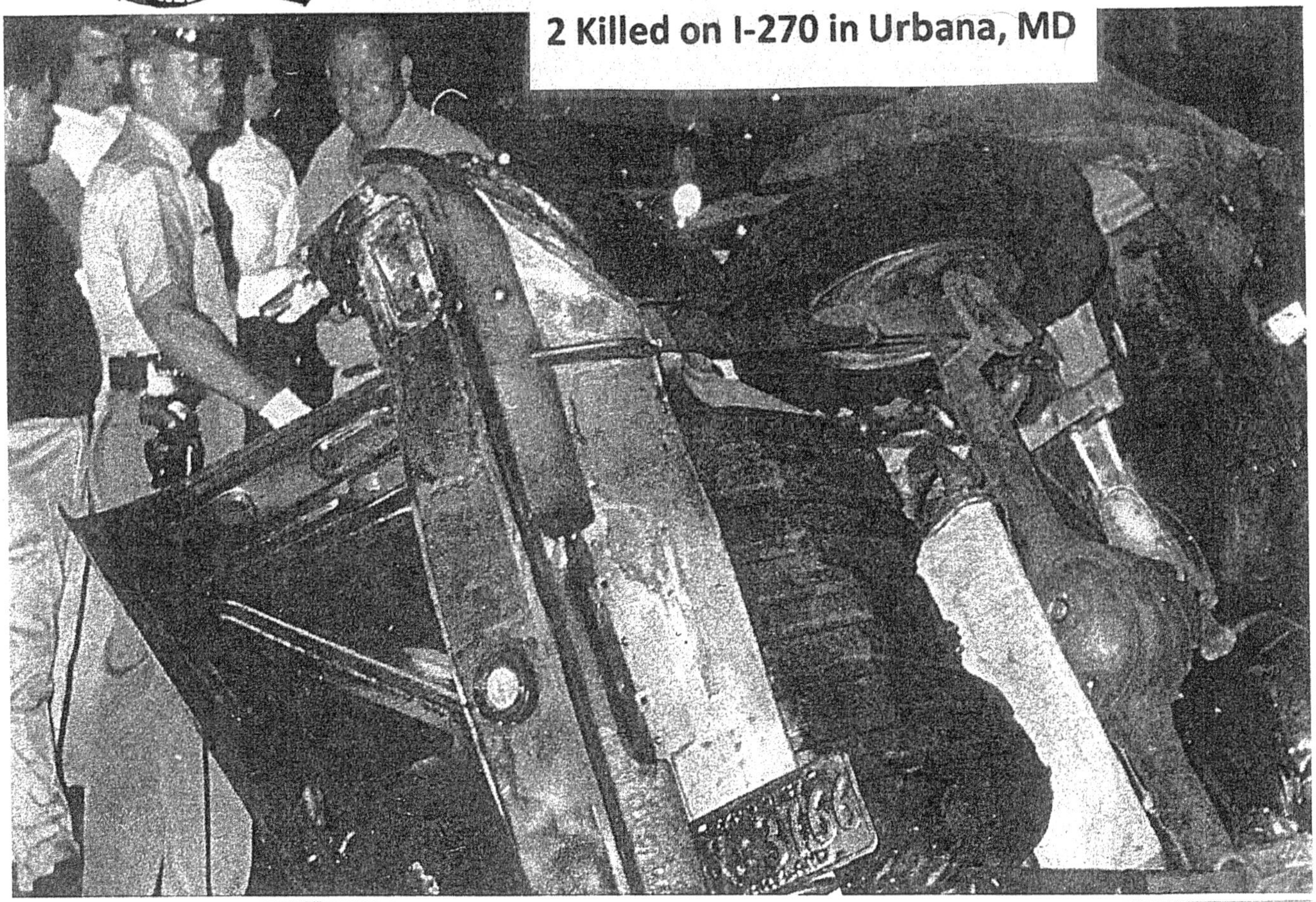

AT THE SITE OF ANOTHER PLANE CRASH IN MARYLAND VICTIM WAS CUT IN HALF

A FATAL WRECK IN ROCKVILLE, IN THE 1970s

CHEESEFINDER WENT TO BOOT HILL TO BUY SOME BOOT'S BUT HE WAS TOLD THAT THE ONLY BOOT'S THERE WERE BURIED ON THE FEET OF DEAD COWBOY'S THAT HAD BEEN PLANTED SO HE LEFT AND WENT TO THE NEARBY MALL

ENGINE COMPANY 82 IN THE SOUTH BRONX-ONE DAY WE WENT ON A SECOND ALARM FIRE THERE RIGHT NEXT TO THEIR FIREHOUSE

A CAR-FULL OF BURNED BODIES ON I-95 DUE TO A WRECK

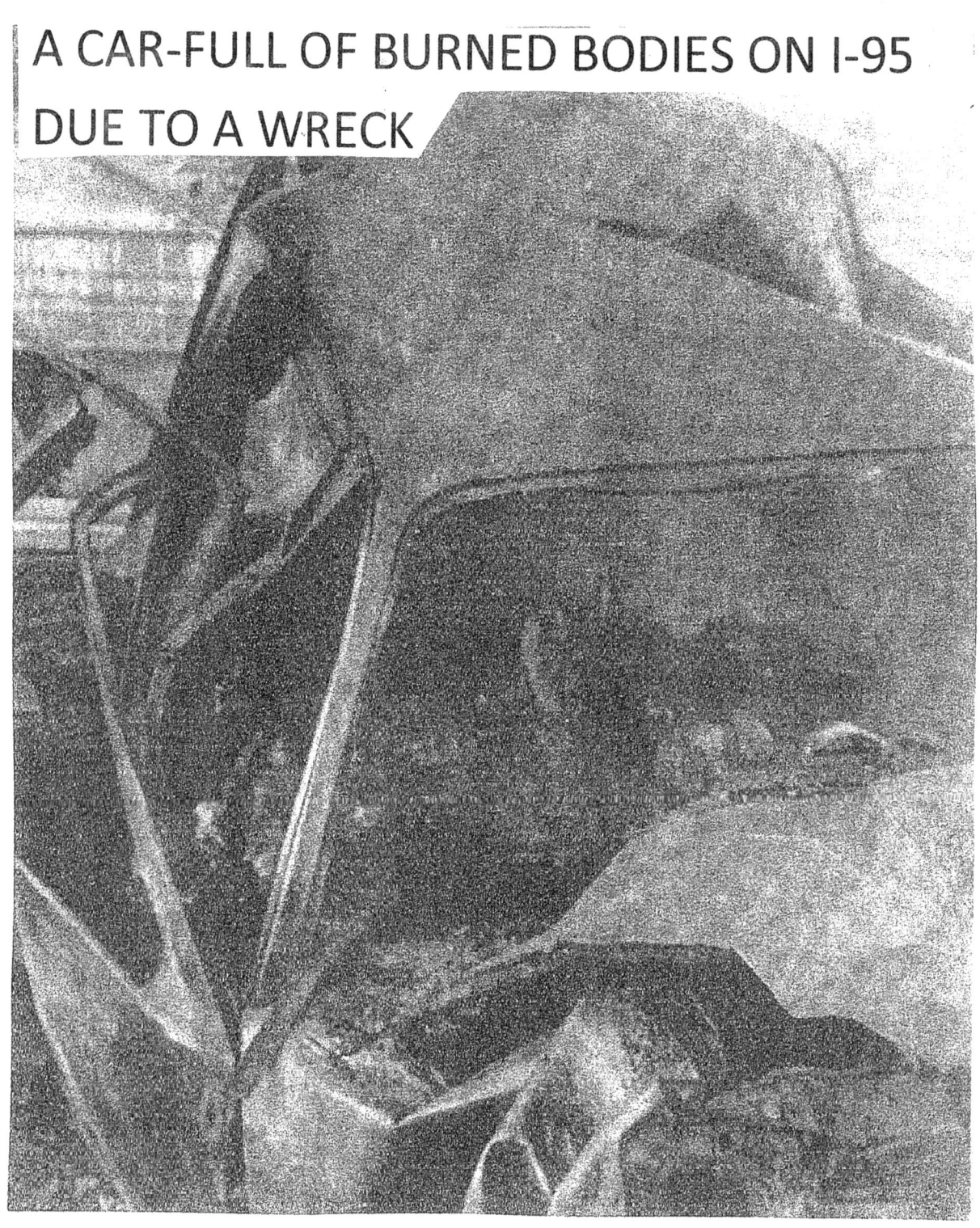

BUILDING DESTROYED IN A 2-ALARM FIRE IN TAKOMA PARK, MD

FIREFIGHTERS IN GAITHERSBURG, MD AT A 4-ALARM FIRE WHERE A TRAIN CAME BY AND SLICED 3 HOSELINES ACROSS THE RR TRACKS

DANNY, JIM BOB, AND JOE HARABSTEIN AT TRIPLE FATAL TRUCK OVERTURNED AT A BUS STOP IN KENSINGTON MD

DANNY WITH AN UNIDENIFIED GORILLA AT A BUILDING FIRE IN LOWER MANHATTAN

3 FELONS BEING CHASED BY DC POLICE ARE KILLED WHEN THEIR CAR OVERTURNS AND CRASHES INTO AN EMBANKMENT

CHEESEFINDER WENT TO BOOT HILL TO BUY SOME BOOT'S BUT HE WAS TOLD THAT THE ONLY BOOT'S THERE WERE BURIED ON THE FEET OF DEAD COWBOY'S THAT HAD BEEN PLANTED SO HE LEFT AND WENT TO THE NEARBY MALL

ENGINE COMPANY 82 IN THE SOUTH BRONX-ONE DAY WE WENT ON A SECOND ALARM FIRE THERE RIGHT NEXT TO THEIR FIREHOUSE

DANNY IN THE USMC, IN SINGAPORE PATTING A MONKEY IN 1958

A car runs into the back of a gasoline tanker and the car explodes killing the driver in the Beltsville area on I-95

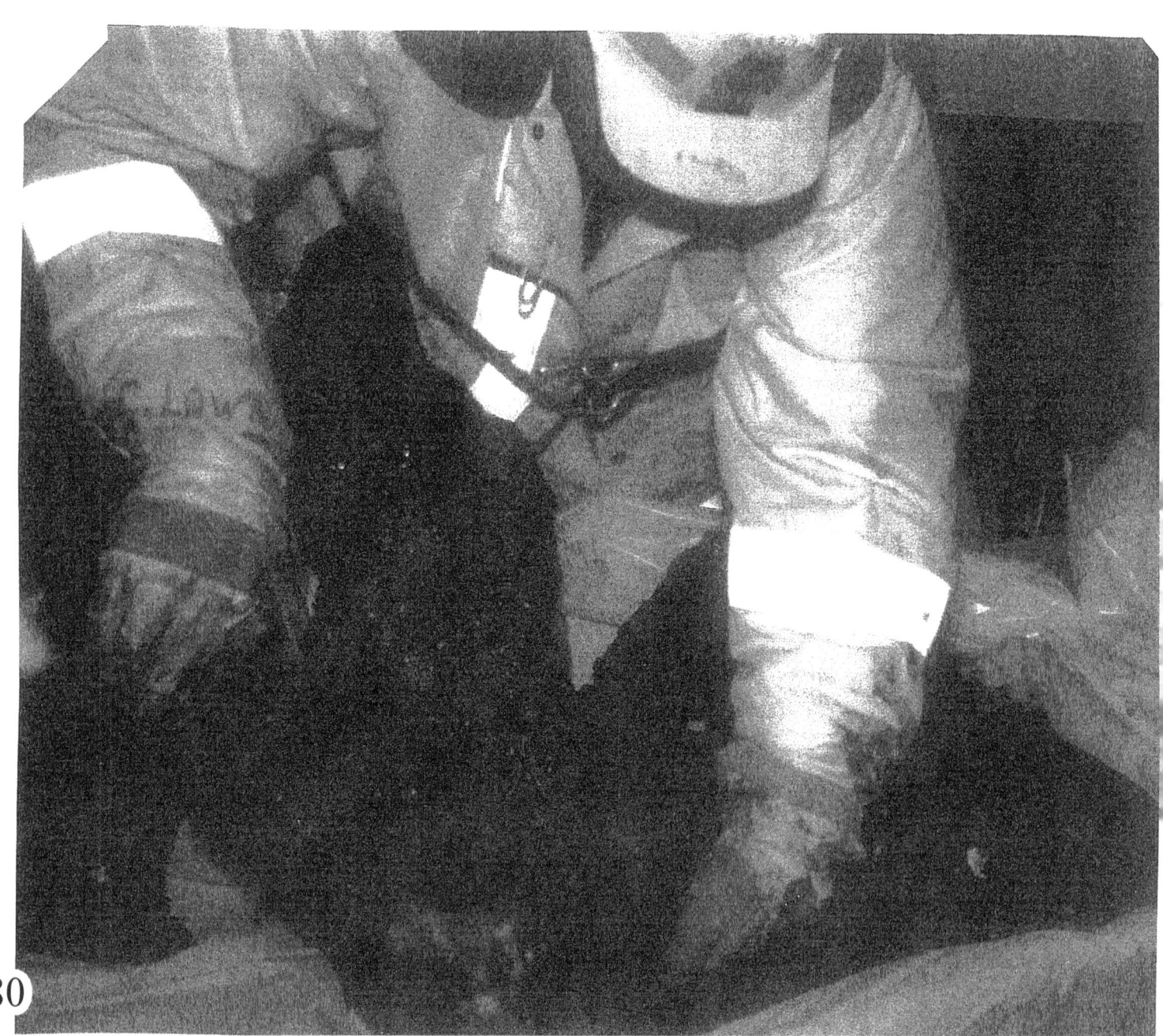

Building Fire in Brooklyn, NY

THIS DUDE DROWNED IN THE POTOMAC RIVER

FREIGHT TRAIN WRECK IN MONTGOMERY COUNTY, MD – A CABOOSE ON TOP OF A ENGINE

A FIRE IN BROOKLYN

A LARGE BUILDING IN BRUNSWICK BURNED DOWN

FATAL PLANE WRECK OVER THE HUDSON RIVER AND FALLING INTO 2 TOWNS

BURNING FREIGHT TRAIN WRECK IN LANDOVER, MD

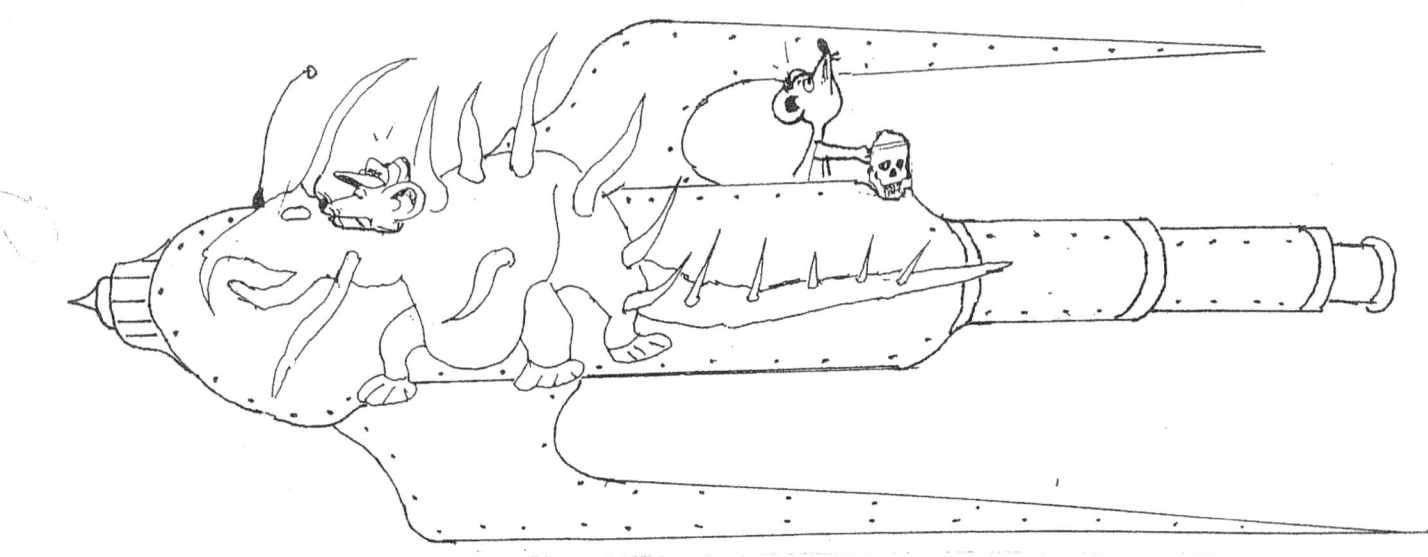

THIS PLANE CRASH IN HOWARD COUNTY MD KILLED 17 PERSONS WHEN THE PLANE A UNITED AIRLINES VISCOUNT CRASHED INTOTHE GROUND

SITE STREWN WITH BODIES OF VICTIMS, CAP, STATE POLICE CONTROL CROWDS AT HORROR SCENE

FATAL DROWNING IN DC IN ANACOSTIA

FATAL APARTMENT FIRE IN THE BRONX, ONE DOG FOUND ALIVE

HOUSE FIRE IN BETHESDA, MD
DOUBLE SUICIDE, VARIOUS ANIMALS SURVIVED

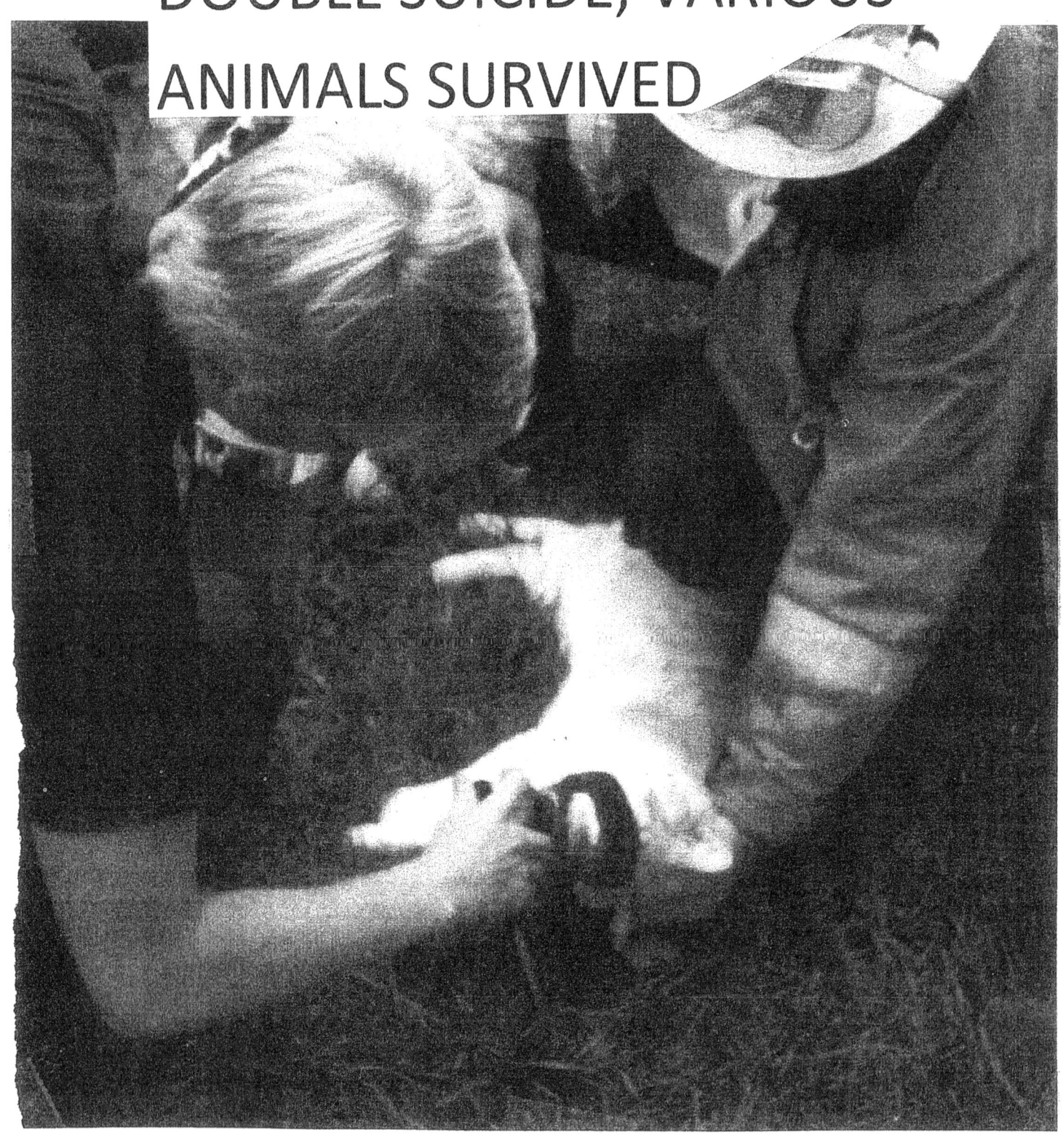

PARK POLICE AND CABIN JOHN FIRE CATS BRINGING IN

ANOTHER WEEK-OLD DROWNING VICTIM

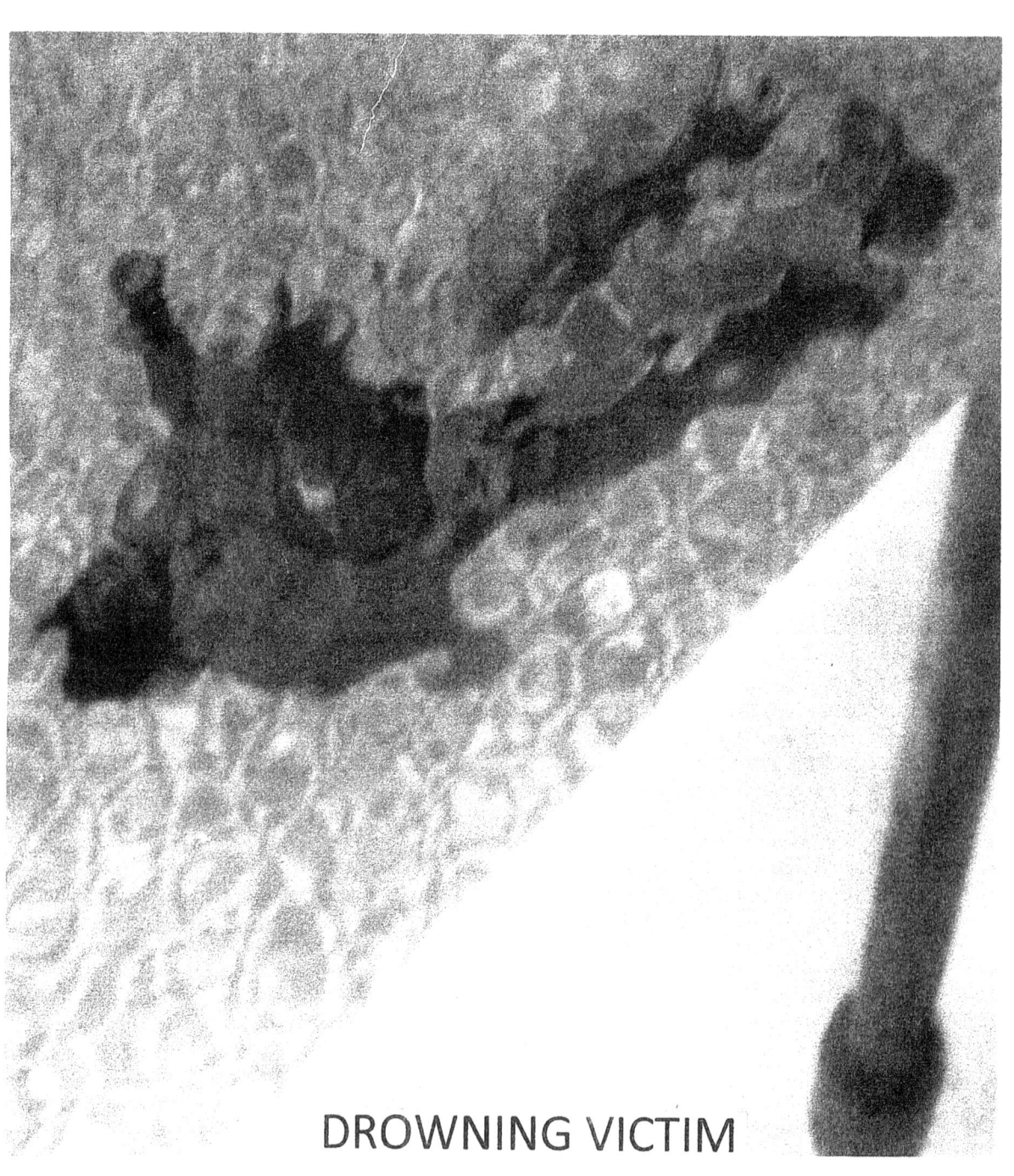

WRECKERS DISMANTLE CHEVY CHASE LANDMARK

Large Fire in Baltimore, MD

TRAIN WRECK IN PG COUNTY WHERE A PRIEST WAS KILLED

DANNY WITH WARREN ISMAN THE HEAD CAT AT A SERIOUS TRAIN WRECK IN GAITHERSBURG

THE BUCKET OF BLOOD BAR IN VIRGINA CITY, NE

The Mice Visit Gulfport, Mississippi after Hurricane Katrina

A FIRE IN MID-TOW MANHATTAN

TRUCK CARRYING PUMPKINS WRECKED KILLING DRIVER ON I-95

A THRIVING BISON RESTURANT

AT A PLANE CRASH IN THE ROCKIES A LONG TIME AGO

IN MONUMENT VALLEY, ARIZONA

A Dog's Prayer

Please do not grieve for me when I am gone from your earthly sphere- and do not make me cry for you. Your tears might spoil my happiness in my new home.

I am reunited with all the other beloved pets that have preceded me to this happy heaven- and there is plenty of space for more.

We will watch over you and love you all forever!

Please believe me.

Penny

By Louise H. Knowles
1995

DISASTERS, FIRES, AND RESCUES 4

THIS PET SNAKE NAMED CHARLES RIDES THE FIRE ENGINE AND MOST OF THE TIME ON THE FRONT BUMPER

BY DANIEL S. KNOWLES

A Plane Crash in Pleasant Valley, MD, Plane Crash at the Montgomery Air Park In Gaithersburg, MD

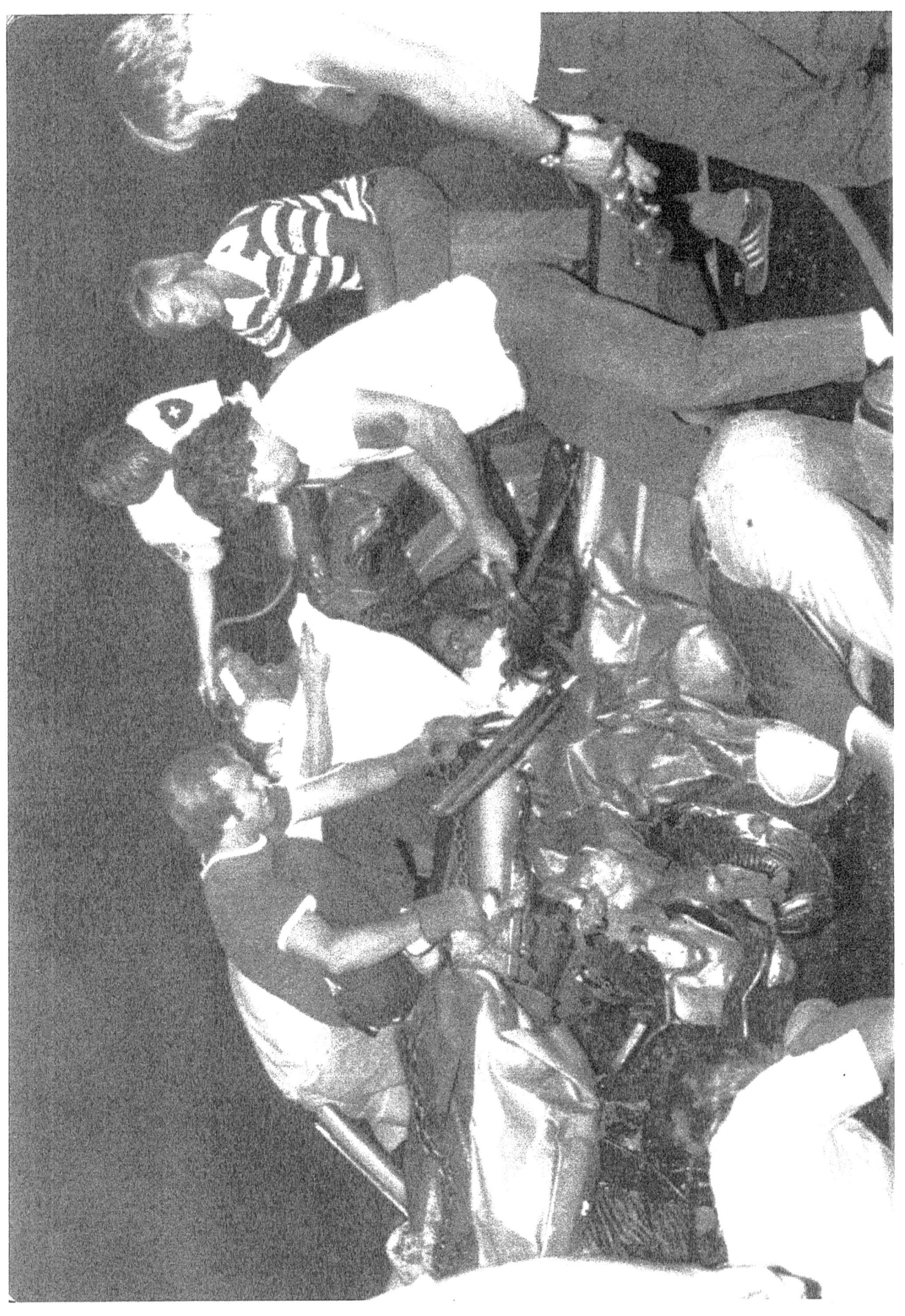

I SERVED OVER 63 YEARS AS A MONTGOMERY COUNTY, MD FIREFIGHTER, DURING THIS TIME I ALSO RODE WITH RESCUE UNITS IN BOSTON AND SPRINGFIELD MASS.

AS WELL AS SOME TIME ON SEVERAL OF THE RESCUE TRUCKS IN EARLY 911 IN NY CITY

I WOULD LIKE TO DEDICATE THIS BOOK IN MEMORY OF THE FIREFIGHTER' WHO HAVE AND WILL GIVE THEIR LIVES BEFORE ME

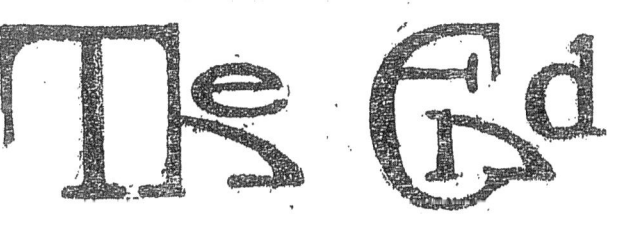

A GOOD-LOOKING

BUFFALO IN SHOCK FROM WHAT HE WAS SEEING

www.ingramcontent.com/pod-product-compliance
Lightning Source LLC
Chambersburg PA
CBHW081716100526
44591CB00016B/2405